P9-CRJ-587

Back to Books

BACK TO BOOKS

200 Library Activities to Encourage Reading

by Karen K. Marshall

CENTRAL MIDDLE SCHOOL
MEDIA CENTER

McFarland 1983

Library of Congress Cataloguing-in-Publication Data

Marshall, Karen K.
  Back to books.

  Bibliography: p.
  Includes index.
  1. School libraries — Activitiy programs. 2. School
children — Library orientation. 3. Children — Books and
reading. 4. Reading games. 5. Library exhibits.
6. Bulletin boards. I. Title.
Z675.S3M2733 1983   025.5′678222   83-42903
ISBN 0-89950-092-7 (pbk.)

© 1983 Karen K. Marshall. All rights reserved.

Manufactured in the United States of America.

*McFarland & Company, Inc., Publishers, Box 611,
  Jefferson, North Carolina 28640*

Table of Contents

Introduction

In developing your library programs, could you use some help in planning games and activities that will add zest to a visit to the school library? *Back to Books: 200 Library Activities to Encourage Reading* was written to fill a need of school librarians and teachers for material to assist them in stimulating an interest in reading for fun. The material includes a few games geared toward teaching library skills. The idea of the book arose from my experience as an elementary school librarian, grades K–8.

This handbook is a collection of new and not-so-new motivational techniques, games, contests, exhibits, bulletin board games, active games and mini-lessons. Comments are given in some instances regarding the children's reactions to the activity.

Success of these library games is evidenced by the frequent fights among the children for who gets to borrow the books mentioned in the program. The Library Media Specialist, as referee, came up with a number game to settle the question of who gets to read the book first. Principals and teachers at my two schools have often commented on the enthusiasm which the children display toward our library activities. Daily statistics of the number of books checked out of our libraries speak for themselves of the popularity of the library, and the interest in and love of reading. Teachers coming from other schools that do not employ librarians have noted that these children are more familiar with books.

Enjoy these games and activities with your children, and go on to create your own.

Part I
Exhibits and Displays

1. Parachuting into Reading

For every book a pupil reads, he is given a parachute with a book attached to it (title, author and call number may be included). These may be displayed in the school hallway or in the library.

2. Travel the Bibliophile Express

With the completion of a book, the student receives a train car with his name and title of book read printed on it. The train car is added on to the last car, and the train may extend quite a long way around the school hallways.

3. Collage

An exhibit may be put in the hallway display case, or book covers may be used to display a number of books on different themes that were taken out of the library the most times in a semester. A brief synopsis may be given of an account of the book.

4. Quest in the Desert

Display titles of books that students would choose to take with them if they were stranded in the desert. Make a bulletin board or a hallway board, and display book titles with pupils' names on construction paper.

5. Paving the Way for Reading

In order to stimulate independent reading, a "Reading Path" can be constructed on the hall wall. As students in the school read a book, a cobblestone may be given to each with their name, grade, class (and title and author of book) on it. They may place the cobblestone on the wall. As the school year progresses, the "Reading Path" grows and grows. Of course, a contest could also be made out of this with the student who reads the most number of books during the school year announced as the winner.

6. Growing Tree

A giant tree is designed, and put on the hallway board, or else one could be placed on the library wall. As a student reads a book, he or she gets a leaf. On the leaf, the student writes name, title of book, author and call number.

7. Foreign Language Authors

This activity would be more appropriate for the high school level than for the elementary grades, although I have used it with 8th grade honor groups. A display of the author's portrait, book, and summary of the title with the original language indicated is featured. Students are to find examples of other authors who have originally written in a foreign tongue.

8. Miniature World

A dollhouse display enhances interest in books of the miniature world. If it is not convenient to display a dollhouse, one could be made by the industrial arts department, or a cardboard house could be designed. Or a simple picture of a house is drawn on the bulletin board. Selected titles about miniature people or dolls could be displayed with index cards and summaries. Suggested titles are: *The Littles* (Peterson); *The Borrowers* (Norton); and *Gulliver's Travels* (Swift).

9. Calendar of Birthdays

The birthdays of authors and illustrators may be observed by presenting a birthday calendar on the bulletin board. The names of birthday authors and illustrators may be kept on the board for the day, or for the week. A sampling of the writer's or artist's work is displayed on a table nearby with some information on the honored person's life along with a brief synopsis on index cards of the books.

10. Books in the Big Top

A tent could be raised in the library in order to display new books that have come in to the library at the beginning of the school year. Or a book fair may be held under the big top in order to raise money for the library. Pictures of clowns and other circus people may be placed around the school and in the library advertising the coming big event.

11. Problems Peep Show

A number of boxes with small openings can be exhibited in the library with labels indicating the topic: conflicts with parents; problems with friends; problems with brothers and sisters; death and dying; going to the hospital; orphans; etc. In each box is presented a number of book summaries that deal with that specific problem.

12. Good Reading Side Show

Prepare a number of boxes with small openings in them. Inside is a bookcover and/or an index card with synopsis. Change the titles every week.

13. Falling Down a Rabbit Hole

A large rabbit hole or shaft is drawn on the bulletin board with an underground scene of *Alice in Wonderland* characters displayed. The characters are holding fantasy titles such as: *The Magic Finger* (Dahl); *The Lion, the Witch and the Wardrobe* (Lewis); *Pinocchio* (Collodi); *James and the Giant Peach* (Dahl); *Winnie-the Pooh* (Milne); *Poor Stainless* (Norton); *The Trumpet of the Swan* (White); and *Charlotte's Web* (White); according to the grade level of reading. The books themselves may be displayed near the bulletin board. Students write comments or observations about the book they read, and these may be tacked on the board.

14. Holiday Cruise

Books featuring islands of the world are presented in an exhibit. Both non-fiction and fiction titles are displayed. A world map is placed on the bulletin board with flag showing the title of each book exhibited.

15. Monsters Menagerie

Exhibit posters and books of the monsters and creatures from mythology as well as other monsters such as Bigfoot or the Loch Ness monster. The librarian may read fragments from the books. Children are always enthusiastic about this subject.

16. Don't Get Caught in Charlotte's Web

A huge spider web is drawn or painted. When a book becomes overdue, the student's name is immediately placed in the web.

17. Supernatural Spectacle

An exhibit of the supernatural: books on ghosts, goblins and witches are featured with interesting quotes displayed on cards. An eerie setting is arranged for effect: cobwebs; a haunted house; skeleton; witch and witch's pot.

18. Grad Bag

During the weeks prior to Christmas, a *grad* bag is organized. Students must have read 25 books in order to be eligible to draw a present from the barrel. Only fiction titles are counted. Small presents may be chosen for the grad bag such as book markers, colored pens and pencils, paperback books, book plates or food gift certificates.

19. Romance Revelry

This exhibit will be of more interest to the girls than the boys. Display a number of teenage stories, romance novels, and growing-up stories. Place cards with catchy tidbits among the books. The girls usually snap them up fast.

20. Fall Festival

Books pertaining to the fall season, such as school stories and football stories, may be displayed. An appropriate background of colored leaves, school posters or pictures from magazines, a one-room schoolhouse made out of cardboard is arranged. A number of 3 x 5 index cards are used to give a short summary of books dealing with the season. Or use old "School Library Journal" summaries or other sources pasted on cards.

21. Sail into Summer

Make a giant sailboat for the bulletin board. A bibliography for good summer reading is put together by the librarian and students with a sentence or two about each book.

22. Self-Understanding Sojourn

Books that help one understand oneself (both fiction and non-fiction) are displayed with brief synopses of the contents. Discussion of the books may encourage reading of other related titles.

23. Literary Map

A map of the United States or the world may be adapted to a literary map where each author or illustrator or book title is pinned to the birthplace, or the place where the book was written or its setting.

24. Machines Come to Life

Machinery personified may be used as a topic of discussion. Some books that serve as its basis are: *Mike Mulligan and His Steam Shovel; the Little Engine That Could; Choo Choo; The Little House;* and *Katy and the Big Snow.* A bulletin board may be displayed using this idea.

25. Believe It or Not

A believe-it-or-not bulletin board features brief facts of world records and phenomenal happenings. Reference is made to the *Guinness Book of World Records* and to the *Guinness Book of Phenomenal Happenings*. Interest in the reference section of the library may be aroused in this way. Students may make up a bulletin board of interesting facts found in other reference books. For example, the *World Almanac* lists all kinds of information.

26. Day to Day Exhibits for the Library Media Center

Each day or each week a different book may be exhibited. Student comments and brief summaries on index cards accompany the exhibit. A different author or illustrator is featured on a bulletin board with biographical information.

27. Friendship Fête

Fiction books that depict friendship are displayed in the hallway display case or in the library along with brief summaries of the stories. Whoever checks out a particular book may be given a special invitation to take part in discussion of the book. A party could be set up in the library.

28. Jump on the Bandwagon

Design a wagon for the hallway board or for the library wall. Every time a student reads a fiction book, she receives a paper book with her name and the title of the book read printed on it. The student then can add a book to the wagon. As soon as the wagon starts to overflow, design another wagon to follow the first one.

29. Book Trek: Travel to Inner Space

A large outline of a profile of a person's head is drawn for the bulletin board. A variety of types of books may be placed nearby with brief summaries. As each student reads a book, a marker may be placed inside the head with an appropriate slogan: for example, "Land of the Giants"; "Land of the Dragons"; "Land of the Rabbits" (for *Watership Down*); "Land of the Imagination" (for *And to Think That I Saw It on Mulberry Street*). The student's name is written on the marker to indicate that he traveled to the Land of the Dragons, for example. This is a class or individual student activity.

30. Ivy League

As each student reads a book, an index card is completed or form filled out indicating that the student has indeed read the book. The librarian then gives the student an ivy leaf giving the student's name and book read to be placed on a vine in the hallway wall. At the end of the school year, the ivy has grown tremendously. In working with the younger grades, some of the children enjoy cutting out and coloring their own ivy leaves.

Part II
Bulletin Board
Games and Dittos

31. Acrostics

This activity consists of a word square in which the words read the same across as down. Book characters or illustrators, or any other category may be used. Students can make up their own. It is also a poem: the first letter of each sentence creates a word.

L   *is for the library*
     a place I especially like to be.

I   *is for the ink with which we do not write*
     on the book which would make an awful sight.

B   *is for the bookmarks that we use*
     to keep our place in the books we choose.

R   *is for relaxing with a good story*
     when I do this I am in my glory.

A   *is for all who enjoy a good book*
     hidden away in our favorite nook.

R   *is for reading and to look*
     at our favorite fiction and picture book.

Y   *is for you and for me*
     we love to go to the library.

32. Table of Contents

The contents pages from 10 to 20 fiction books are typed on colored paper or on index cards, and displayed on the bulletin board. Students must determine from which book each *Contents* was taken and put their answers in an enclosed receptacle along with their name, class and grade. The student who guesses the most titles wins. A prize may be given. Posted announcements or bulletins over the intercom or even the local radio station also give the student the great satisfaction of being the winner of a contest. This game is designed for grades 5-up.

33. What Magazine Is Suggested By?

This is a ditto passed out to each student in the class. Students must familiarize themselves with the library's collection of magazines to answer these. Students enjoy doing it.

A fast car? HOT ROD
Fixing cars? POPULAR MECHANICS
A Young Lady? YOUNG MISS
A Nursery Rhyme? JACK AND JILL or HUMPTY DUMPTY
Hunting and fishing? FIELD AND STREAM
Features for children? HIGHLIGHTS FOR CHILDREN
A tutor? INSTRUCTOR or TEACHER
Information bulletin? NEWSWEEK or U.S. NEWS & WORLD REPORT
Peruser's directory? READERS' GUIDE
Child's existence? BOYS LIFE or CHILD LIFE
Black? EBONY
Kid's summary? CHILDREN'S DIGEST
Buyer's summary? CONSUMER REPORTS
Outside being? OUTDOOR LIFE
Fast two-wheeler? CYCLE
Peruser's summary? READER'S DIGEST
Verifiable summary? SCIENCE DIGEST
Teenage? SEVENTEEN
Winter sport? SKIING

Games with pictures? SPORTS ILLUSTRATED
Duration? TIME
Existence? LIFE
Kindred well-being? FAMILY HEALTH
A jumping insect? CRICKET
Currency? MONEY

34. Climb the Mountain

A "Climb the Mountain" ditto is made with steps to the top. Each step is a type of book: historical fiction; science fiction; fantasy; a non-fiction book on a country; a biography; a fairy tale; and a folk tale. As the student climbs one step at a time, and reaches the top, he receives a mountain climber's medallion. Each student may keep dittos in a library folder in his desk, to be taken to the library during a class visit.

35. Mystery Question

Twenty-five questions are posted on the bulletin board. The librarian selects one of the 25 questions to be the secret mystery question so that the student who chooses to answer that question wins a prize. Students select one or more questions to answer when they visit the library. They write their answers on a brief form which they pick up near the bulletin board, and drop the forms into an enclosed receptacle. Questions may pertain to reference books or fiction books in the library. The student who selects the mystery question, and answers it correctly, wins a small prize.

36. What Happens Next?

This bulletin board display features index cards with brief summaries of a number of fiction books without the endings being revealed. Students must read the books to find out the endings, and whoever reads all of the listed selections wins a prize. The student who reads all the selections must present the librarian with an index card or sheet of paper with the endings of the stories presented as proof that he has read all the books. Since only one person can take a specific copy out of the library at a time, the library should own a number of copies of books used in this activity. For example, we have at least five copies of *Charlotte's Web*. Students may venture to the public library to borrow a book.

37. Famous Quotations

A "Famous Quotation" bulletin board features numbered quotations from Bartlett's with the heading: "Who Said It?" Students must use the reference book in order to find the source of each quote. The librarian gives a ditto of the contents of the bulletin board to each pupil. In their spare time, students are to search for the answers. The pupil who finds the most answers in the shortest time may win a small prize. Or, students coming to the library on an individual basis may find the answers, and submit the completed numbered form into a receptacle. Each student who correctly completes the exercise may receive a colored pencil, a bookmark, or other small prize.

38. Indy 500 Road Race

Mount a racetrack with cars on a wall or bulletin board. Along the track are various types of reading: science fiction; fantasy; historical fiction; picture books; humorous stories; friendship; sports stories; fairy tales; etc. The idea of this race is to see which class can get to the finish line first. In order to prevent students from faking, the teacher of the class can determine whether or not the pupil has read the book by having the students write a brief summary of it. To participate in the race, a student "drives" from category to category, reading one title in each, until the finish line is crossed.

39. Caldecott Award Winners Match

Dry mount and laminate a series of illustrations from discarded books, or from publisher's catalogs. Mount these on a bulletin board along with the titles and authors of books (made out of construction paper, and tacked on the board). The correct title must be placed under the corresponding illustration. Grades 1–3 can try to make a perfect score as they visit the library. The class who matches all the titles with the illustrations is the winner, and should be given a prize.

40. Match Author to Book Synopsis — Character or Setting

On the bulletin board place a number of book titles of a featured author on one side, and a brief synopsis of each book on the other side. Students must match the books with the synopses. Students become familiar with a particular author's works even though they do not necessarily read every book. Use index cards with tacks or other materials.

41. Read the Paragraph by Decoding

A B C D E F G H I J K L M N O P Q R S T U V W X Y Z

. . . .

Z Y X W V U T S R Q P O N M L K J I H G F E D C B A

1 2 3 4 5 6 7 8 9

. . . .

9 8 7 6 5 4 3 2 1

GSV YLLPH RM LFI ORYIZIB ZIV XOZHHRURVW YB GSV WVDVB WVXRNZO HBHGVN XOZHHRURXZGRLM. GSRH HBHGVN XOZHHRURVH ZOO PMLDOVWTV RMGL 89 XOZHHVH, 900-000. BLF DROO URMW SRHGLIB YLLPH RM GSV 099 XOZHH, ZMW UZRIB GZOVH RM GSV 699 XOZHH.

The books in our library are classified by the Dewey Decimal System of Classification. This system classifies all knowledge into 10 classes, 000-999. You will find history books in the 900 class, and fairy tales in the 300 class.

42. Literary Lore

Each class member is given a ditto sheet with written questions pertaining to the works of one author or illustrator, or of many authors and titles. Whoever finishes first with all the answers correct wins this game.

Judy Blume

The book that inquires of His presence? *Are You There God? It's Me Margaret.*

The book that is the opposite of slim? *(Blubber)*

The book that rhymes with teeny? *(Deenie)*

The book that has spots all over? *(Freckle Juice)*

The book that says the opposite of beginning or creation? *(It's Not the End of the World)*

The book that speaks of a girl's name rather than the true name? *(Otherwise Known as Sheila the Great)*

The book that has a star in it? *(Starring Sally J. Freedman as Herself)*

The book that makes you hungry? *(Superfudge)*

The book that spins stories of an elementary grade student? *(Tales of a Fourth Grade Nothing)*

The book that can't make up its mind? *(Then Again, Maybe I Won't)*

Scott O'Dell

The book that is the opposite of white; with costume jewelry attached? *(Black Pearl)*

The book that is the opposite of free? *(Captive)*

The book that rhymes with Grenada? *(Carlotta)*

The book that is a youngster of flames? *(Child of Fire)*

The book that is a boat trip of the opposite of antarctic star? *(Cruise of the Arctic Star)*

The book that is a boat that reflects no light? *(Dark Canoe)*

The book that is a covered snake? *(Feathered serpent)*

The book that is a vacation spot? *(Island of the Blue Dolphins)*

The book that asks nicely to do something? *(Kathleen, Please Come Home)*

The book that is a proper name? *(Sarah Bishop)*

The book that is the opposite of talk up the sun? *(Sing Down the Moon)*

The book that is the opposite of trash? *(Treasure of Topo-el-Bampo)*

The book that is one less than two-hundred ninety-one? *(290)*

The book that rhymes with Mia? *(Zia)*

43. Initialed Authors

Each student is given a ditto sheet on which are written groups of words that are descriptive of an author, and with each word having the same first letter as the author's initials, in proper sequence. The student who guesses the most authors wins the game. One may use titles of books or book characters instead of authors. Older students are better suited for this activity, and they may use the card catalog or browse in the library in order to find the answers.

Mirthful Tale-sketcher MARK TWAIN
Wary Sage WILLIAM SHAKESPEARE
Venerable Hero VICTOR HUGO
Laborious Talker LEO TOLSTOI
Not Happy-go-lucky NATHANIEL HAWTHORNE
All-out Debauchery ALEXANDER DUMAS
Joyous Babble JUDY BLUME
High-spirited Charismatic Acquaintance   HANS CHRISTIAN
   ANDERSEN
Winning Teacher WILLIAM THACKERAY
Accomplished Transcriber ALFRED TENNYSON
Jubilant Satirist JONATHAN SWIFT
Bubbly Celebrity BETTY CAVANNA
Just Character JAMES COOPER
Brilliant Hokum BRET HARTE
Jocular Speaker JOHANNA SPYRI

44. Book Bingo

Children like bingo, and it can be a great way to familiarize
them with titles, authors, and illustrators. The activity can certainly
be varied and adapted in numerous ways for the library. Make
BINGO cards, and always laminate them so you will get more use
out of them. Label the columns PICTURE BOOK, FICTION, NON-
FICTION, MYSTERY, BIOGRAPHY, AUTHOR or anything you like.
Assemble a list of at least 10 to 12 or more answers in each classification. Write in the titles or names on the cards in various orders.
You call the names and titles instead of numbers in random order.
Prizes can be given. Or just use three categories such as book char-
acters, titles, and authors for the lower grades as shown next page.

Title	Character	Author	Title	Character
Jennie's Hat	Lucille	Ezra Jack Keats	Quito Express	Chester
Madeline	Petunia	Virginia Burton	Chanticleer the Fox	Veronica
Anansi the Spider	Anatole	Roger Duvoisin	The Snowy Day	Frederick
Pet Show	Curious George	Ludwig Bemelmans	Loopy	Gingerbread Man
Fish Is Fish	Swimmy	Leo Lionni	Blue Bug to the Rescue	Babar
Blueberries For Sal	Mike Mulligan	Marie Hall Ets	In the Forest	Little Bear
Maggie the Pirate	Horton	Dr. Seuss	And to Think That I Saw It on Mulberry St.	Crocus
One Fine Day	Jasmine	Marjorie Flack	Angus Lost	Beppolino
The Little House	Sam	Bettina	No, Agatha	Bangs
Andy and the Lion	Max	Beatrix Potter	Hi, Cat	George and Martha
The Little Island	Oliver	Don Freeman	The Mighty Hunter	Obadiah
Mine	Peter	Rachel Isadora	Milton the Early Riser	Willie

45. Good Things Come in Small Packages

Each time a student reads a book with the word "little" in the title, the student's name and book title is placed on a bulletin board on colored construction paper in the shape of a gift with yarn or ribbons or other decorations to make the "gift" attractive. Below are listings of book titles with the word "little."

Grades 1–3

Little Black, a Pony (Farley)
The Little House (Burton)
The Little Island (MacDonald)
Little Toot (Gramatky)
Little Monkey (Thayer)
Little Pieces of the West Wind (Garrison)
Little Quack (Woods)
Little Nora (Wells)
Little Ghost Godfrey (Sandberg)
Little Silk (Ayer)
Little Bear's Friend (Minarik)
Little bear's Visit (Minarik)
Little Bear (Minarik)
Little Auto (Lenski)
Little Airplane (Lenski)
Little Train (Lenski)
Little Boy and the Giant (Harrison)
Little Black Puppy (Zolotow)
Little Brown Bear and His Friends (Upham)
Little Brown Horse (Otto)
Little Cat That Could Not Sleep (Fox)
Little Chief (Hoff)
Little Cowboy (Brown)
Little Crow (Osswald)
A Little Dog Called Kitty (Thayer)
Little Drummer Boy (Keats)
Little Elephant's Christmas (Washburne)

The Little Engine That Could (Piper)
The Little Engine That Laughed (Evers)
Little Fat Gretchen (Brock)
Little Fireman (Brown)
Little Frightened Tiger (MacDonald)
Little Fu (Creekmore)
Little Fur Family (Brown)
Little Lulu and the Magic Paints (Drake)
Little Old Automobile (Ets)
The Little Old Train (Otto)

Little Owl Indian (Beatty)
Little Park (Fife)
Little Puff (Hillert)
Little Red Hen (Berg)
Little Red Nose (Schlein)
Little Runaway (Hillert)
Little Runner of the Longhouse (Baker)
Little Wild Horse (Beatty)
Little Woman Who Forgot Everything (Beattie)
Little Wooden Farmer (Dalgliesh)
Littlest Witch (Massey)
Little Peep (Kent)

Grades 4-6

Little House in the Big Woods (Wilder)
Little Women (Alcott)
Little Men (Alcott)
Stuart Little (White)
Little House on the Prairie (Wilder)
Little Brother, No More (Benton)

Little Brown Bear Goes to School (Upham)
Little Indian Basketmaker (Clark)
Little Indian Pottery Maker (Clark)
Little Maverick Cow (Coates)
Little Navajo Bluebird (Wilder)
Little Town on the Prairie (Wilder)
The Littles (Peterson)
Little Destiny (Cleaver)
Little Girl Lost (Bolton)

46. Decode the Title

The code titles may be placed on the bulletin board or used with dittos, with separate answer sheets. For grades 4–6.

Code:

A B C D E F G H I J K L M N O P Q R S T U V W X Y Z
. . . .
Z Y X W V U T S R Q P O N M L K J I H G F E D C B A

HVZ HGZI LIKSZM LU XSRMXLGVZTFV *Sea Star Orphan of Chincoteague* (Henry)

DZGVIHSRK WLDM *Watership Down* (Adams)

KRIZGV'S KILNRHV *Pirate's Promise* (Bulla)

GSV OZHG LU GSV NLSRXZMH *The Last of the Mohicans* (Cooper)

GSV YOZXP HGZOORLM'H HFOPB XLOG *The Black Stallion's Sulky Colt* (Farley)

GSV SRTS PRMT *The High King* (Alexander)

UREV ORGGOV KVKKVIH ZMW SLD GSVB TIVD *Five Little Peppers and How They Grew* (Sidney)

DRGXS LU GSV XFNYVIOZMWH *(Witch of the Cumberlands)* (Stephens)

GSV MLLMWZB UIRVMWH *The Noonday Friends* (Stolz)

NLOOB GSV ILTFV *Molly the Rogue* (Walsh)

UFIB LM HPZGVH *Fury on Skates* (Honig)

XOFVH RM GSV DLLWH *Clues in the Woods* (Parish)

IZNLMZ *Ramona* (Jackson)

ZWZN LU GSV ILZW *Adam of the Road* (Gray)

KRKKR OLMTHGLXPRMT *Pippi Longstocking* (Lindgren)

RHOZMW LF GSV YOFV WLOKSRMH *Island of the Blue Dolphins* (O'Dell)

NLYB WRXP *Moby Dick* (Melville)

...ZMW MLD NRTFVO *...And Now Miguel* (Krumgold)

NBHGVIB LU GSV NZBZ QZWV *Mystery of the Maya Jade* (Honness)

GRNV XZG *Time Cat* (Alexander)

ILDZM UZIN *Rowan Farm* (Benary-Isbert)

GSV HVXIVG TZIWVM *The Secret Garden* (Burnett)

GSV HFNNVI LU GSV HDZMH *The Summer of the Swans* (Byars)

ZKIRO'H DRGXSVH *April's Witches* (Crook)

GSV GLNYH LU ZGFZM *The Tombs of Atuan* (Le Guin)

47. Code Telegram

Grades 4–6

	BOOK CHARACTER	BOOK TITLE	AUTHOR
L	Laurie	*Little Women*	Lamorisse
I	Ivanhoe	*Iron Cage*	Washington Irving
B	Betsy	*Black Pearl*	Frank Bonham
R	Ribsy	*Ramona, the Brave*	Marjorie Rawlings
A	Alice in Wonderland	*Adam of the Road*	Louisa May Alcott
R	Rufus	*Runaway Ralph*	Glen Rounds
Y	Yonie Wondernose	*Yearling*	Jane Yolen
B	Blubber	*Bad Times of Irma Baumlein*	Betsy Byars
O	Oliver Twist	*Of Mice and Men*	Scott O'Dell
O	Onion John	*Of Human Bondage*	Helen Orton
K	Kristie	*King of the Wind*	Rudyard Kipling
S	Socks	*The Saturdays*	Margaret Sidney

Grades 1-3

	BOOK CHARACTER	BOOK TITLE	AUTHOR
L	Lucille	*Loopy*	Leo Lionni
I	Izzie	*Inch by Inch*	Rachel Isadora
B	Broderick	*Bedtime for Frances*	Clyde Robert Bulla
R	Red fox	*Runaway Bunny*	H.A. Rey
A	Anatole	*Anansi the Spider*	Joan Walsh Anglund
R	Raggedy Ann	*Rosie's Walk*	Ann and Paul Rand
Y	Yeck eck yetta	*Yertle the Turtle*	Ylla
B	Babar	*Big Snow*	Virginia Lee Burton
O	Obadiah	*Olly's polliwogs*	Lucy Ozone
O	Orlando	*Oscar Otter*	Margaret Otto
K	Katy no-pocket	*King's Stilts*	Ezra Jack Keats
S	Sneakers	*Sam, Bangs and Moonshine*	Maurice Sendak

48. Biblical Places Match

S	ARARAT	V	EPHESUS
Z	BABEL	X	ESDRAELON, PLAIN OF
I	BABYLON	P	GALATIA
N	BETHEL	C	GALILEE
Y	BETHESDA, POOL OF	L	GATH
U	BETHLEHEM	E	GAZA
H	CITIES OF REFUGE	Q	GEHENNA
R	CORINTH	A	GETHSEMANE
B	DAMASCUS	M	GILEAD
G	DEAD SEA	J	ISRAEL
D	EDEN	W	JERUSALEM
K	EDOM	T	JORDAN RIVER
O	EGYPT, ANCIENT	F	JUDEA

A A place on the Mount of Olives away from the hustle and bustle of Jerusalem. Where Judas came to betray Jesus.

B When Paul made the journey from Jerusalem to this place, the capital of Syria, to persecute the Christians, but instead he preached their faith in the synagogue.

C Land of Jesus Christ's boyhood and place of his beginning ministry.

D A beautiful place where Adam and Eve lived.

E Joshua captured this city from the Philistines.

F Name of the country in the southern part of Palestine in ancient times. Named for the tribe of Judah.

G Anyone who tries to swim in it just floats. There is so much salt and other chemicals in this body of water that fish cannot live in it.

H   A man who accidentally killed another man could be safe here, at least for the time being.

I   One of the wonder cities of the ancient world. Its famous king was Nebuchadnezzar.

J   The new name given to Jacob which means *God strives*. Also, the Promised Land.

K   This word means *red*.

L   One of five main cities of the Philistines, and home of the giant, Goliath.

M   Places on the east side of the River Jordan with hills used as hiding places for fugitives.

N   Where Abraham built an altar to God.

O   Had powerful Pharaoh-Kings, famous buildings and civilization.

P   Now a part of Turkey. Paul wrote famous letter to the Galatians.

Q   Sacrifice of children took place there. Place became a symbol of hell.

R   One of the most important cities of ancient Greece. St. Paul founded a church here.

S   A volcano where Noah's Ark came to rest after the flood.

T   The most famous river in the Bible. Jesus was baptized in it by John.

U   Birthplace of Jesus.

V   Was a famous seaport and center of worship of the goddess, Diana. It is now a collection of ruined buildings.

W   Means *peace*. David captured the city and made it a capitol.

X   A fertile plain through which the important east-west road runs from the Jordan to the Mediterranean.

Y   Healing waters in Jerusalem.

Z   A city where no one could understand anyone else because no one spoke the same language.

49. Match Theme with Book

One way to present this game is on dittos, in two columns: one lists titles (with authors) and the other assorted subjects, scrambled from the order below.

Grades 4–6

Chaotic Kitchen (Weir) TEEN-AGE LIFE
Mills Down Below (Allan) WOMEN'S RIGHTS
Charmed Life (Jones) WITCHES AND MAGIC
What's Best for You (Angell) DIVORCE
Tucker and the Horse Thief (Terris) FRONTIER AND PIONEER LIFE
The Summer of the Swans (Byars) ADOLESCENCE
Edgar Allan (Neufeld) ADOPTION
Dave White and the Electric Wonder Car (Butterworth) COLLEGE
A Toad for Tuesday (Erickson) FRIENDSHIP
Joyride (Cavanna) PHYSICALLY HANDICAPPED
Empty Seat (Green) DEATH
North of Danger (Fife) WAR
Dead Man's Light (Corbett) ORPHANS
Tuned Out (Wojciechowska) DRUGS
Bonnie Jo, Go Home (Eyerly) ABORTION
A Breath of Fresh Air (Cavanna) DIVORCE
My Robot Buddy (Slote) FRIENDSHIP
Kate's Story (Leach) JUVENILE DELINQUENCY
Magic Moth (Lee) DEATH

c/o Arnold's Corners (Newton) PREJUDICES
My Brother is Stevie (Clymer) PROBLEM CHILDREN
Green Street (Arundel) SOCIAL PROBLEMS
Dumb Like Me, Olivia Potts (Perl) FRIENDSHIP
Shadow Guests (Aiken) GHOST STORIES
Across Five Aprils (Hunt) SLAVERY AND CIVIL WAR

50. Match Detective with Mystery

The Hound of the Baskervilles SHERLOCK HOLMES
The Clue of the Hissing Serpent HARDY BOYS
The Forest Adventure BOBBSEY TWINS
The Musgrave Ritual SHERLOCK HOLMES
The Case of the Midnight Visitor ENCYCLOPEDIA BROWN
Footprints Under the Window HARDY BOYS
A Study in Scarlet SHERLOCK HOLMES
A Scandal in Bohemia SHERLOCK HOLMES
The Red-headed League SHERLOCK HOLMES
The Ghost at Skeleton Rock HARDY BOYS
The Sign of the Four SHERLOCK HOLMES
Danger on Vampire Trail HARDY BOYS
The Adventure of the Speckled Band SHERLOCK HOLMES
The Jungle Pyramid HARDY BOYS
Silver Blaze SHERLOCK HOLMES
The Adventure of the Blue Carbuncle SHERLOCK HOLMES
Mystery of the Samurai Sword HARDY BOYS
The Secret Agent on Flight 101 HARDY BOYS
The Secret of Skull Mountain HARDY BOYS
The Sting of the Scorpion HARDY BOYS
The Play House Secret BOBBSEY TWINS
The Blue Poodle Mystery BOBBSEY TWINS
The Message in the Hollow Oak NANCY DREW
The Mystery at Lilac Inn NANCY DREW
The Mystery of the Brass Bound Trunk NANCY DREW
The Mystery of the Ivory Charm NANCY DREW
Mystery of the Moss-covered Mansion NANCY DREW
Mystery of the 99 Steps NANCY DREW
The Secret in the Old Attic NANCY DREW

The Spider Sapphire Mystery NANCY DREW
— — — *Lends a Hand* ENCYCLOPEDIA BROWN
— — — *Solves Them All* ENCYCLOPEDIA BROWN
Secret at Shadow Ranch NANCY DREW

51. Newbery Honor Award Match

This bulletin board activity consists of looking up titles and authors in the card catalog. The class is given a specified time limit to finish the task. The classes (grades 5 and 6) may compete for fastest time. The students must place the correct author and summary under the correct title by pins or tacks.

52. Mystery Match

A Arthur Conan Doyle
B Dorothy Sayers
C Agatha Christie
D Mary Roberts Rinehart
E George Simenon

C *The Body in the Library*
A *The Land of Mist*
B *Whose Body?*
D *The Circular Staircase*
C *Murder in the Calais Coach*
E *The Crime of Inspector Maigret*
A *The Hound of the Baskervilles*
D *Two Flights Up*

C   *The Patriotic Murders*
E   *The Strange Case of Peter the Lett*
B   *Murder must Advertise*
D   *The Amazing Interlude*
A   *The Maracot Deep*
E   *The Death of M. Gallet*
B   *Have His Carcass*
E   *Affairs of Destiny*
A   *The Case-book of Sherlock Holmes*
C   *Evil Under the Sun*
B   *The Mind of the Maker*
D   *The Wall*
D   *The Amazing Adventures of Letitia Carberry*
A   *The Great Boer War*
B   *Lord Peter Views the Body*
C   *Boomerang Clue*
E   *The Crossroad Murders*

53. Historical Fiction Guess Chronology

Listen, the Drum (Alter) COLONIAL, 1732–1799
Time of the Tomahawk (Alter) COLONIAL, 1763–1765
Two Sieges of the Alamo (Alter) PIONEER, 1836
The Totem Casts a Shadow (Bell) PIONEER
The Ark (Benary-Isbert) WORLD WAR II
Rowan Farm (Benary-Isbert) WORLD WAR II
Stranded (Burchard) PIONEER, 1875
Pilgrim Kate (Daringer) PILGRIMS
The Robe (Douglas) 30 B.C. to 47 A.D.
The Wind Blows Free (Erdman) PIONEER, 1890's
Johnny Tremain (Forbes) AMERICAN REVOLUTION
The Snow Goose (Gallico) WORLD WAR II
Moccasin Trial (McGraw) PIONEER
Magnificent Mutineers (Miers) REVOLUTION
The Bronze Bow (Speare) FIRST CENTURY
Calico Captive (Speare) COLONIAL, FRENCH & INDIAN WAR
    1754–1763

The Witch of Blackbird Pond (Speare) COLONIAL
Uncle Tom's Cabin (Stowe) CIVIL WAR
Morgan's Long Rifles (Taylor) REVOLUTION
John Treegate's Muskat (Wibberley) COLONIAL
Peter Treegate's War (Wibberly) REVOLUTION
Sea Captain from Salem (Wibberley) REVOLUTION
Treegate's Raiders (Wibberley) REVOLUTION
Secret of Van Rink's Cellar (Lee) REVOLUTION & WAR OF 1812
Rifles for Watie (Keith) CIVIL WAR

54. Fiction Classic Match

A	SEWELL		M	STEVENSON
B	WILLIAMS		N	CRANE
C	ALCOTT		O	SHELLEY
D	BARRIE		P	CARROLL
E	ANDERSEN		Q	GRAHAME
F	RAWLINGS		R	HODGSON
G	SPYRI		S	SIDNEY
H	DICKENS		T	KIPLING
I	HUGO		U	LONDON
J	COLLODI		V	TWAIN
K	VERNE		W	BRONTE
L	MACDONALD		X	MELVILLE
		Y	BURNETT	

C   *Little Men*
J   *Adventures of Pinocchio*
S   *Five Little Peppers and How They Grew*
E   *Andersen's Fairy Tales*
M   *Treasure Island*
P   *Through the Looking Glass*
D   *Peter Pan*
K   *Around the World in Eighty Days*
G   *Heidi*
B   *Velveteen Rabbit*
Y   *The Secret Garden*
X   *Moby Dick*

O *Frankenstein*
V *The Prince and the Pauper*
U *Call of the Wild*
L *At the Back of the North Wind*
H *Tale of Two Cities*
N *Red Badge of Courage*
R *Little Princess*
A *Black Beauty*
W *Jane Eyre*
Q *Wind in the Willows*
T *The Jungle Book*
F *The Yearling*
I *Les Miserables*

55. Monster Match

H	ARGUS	L	GRIFFIN
D	CENTAUR	N	HARPY
O	CERBERUS	B	HYDRA
J	CHIMERA	G	MEDUSA
F	CYCLOPS	C	MINOTAUR
M	GIANT	K	PEGASUS
A	GORGON	E	PHOENIX
	I. UNICORN		

A Three terrible beings who had snakes on their heads instead of hair; anyone who looked at their faces turned to stone.

B A nine-headed serpent

C Had head of a bull and body of a man.

D A creature that was half man and half horse.

E A bird with brilliant gold and reddish-purple feathers who lived 500 years, and then burned itself on a funeral pyre.

F   A giant shepherd who had one eye in the center of his forehead.

G   One of the three Gorgons with staring eyes, protruding fangs and snakes for hair.

H   He had 100 eyes.

I   Looked like a horse, and on the forehead had a horn with a spiral twist.

J   Fire-breathing with head of a lion and tail of a dragon.

K   A winged horse.

L   Had head and wings of an eagle and body of a lion.

M   Looked like a man, but much larger in size.

N   Half bird and half woman.

O   A three-headed dog who guarded the gate of Hades.

56. What's Wrong with This?

In the listings below, the title and author are followed by a one sentence synopsis, with something wrong. For younger grades you may want to underline the incorrect word or phrase. The correct word is in parentheses.

Grades 1–3

The Egg Tree, Milhous. Katy and Carl spent a wonderful Easter on an **African** farm. (Pennsylvania)

Angus Lost, Flack. I am a **big bird** with a big curiosity. (Little terrier dog)

Bettina, Pantaloni. Beppolino, a small Italian boy, tries to find his lost **monkey**. (Dog)

Millions of Cats, Gag. When the very old man went to look for a little kitten to bring home to his very old wife, **he couldn't find any.** (Found millions of cats)

Petunia, Duvoisin. Petunia was a very silly **mouse**. (Goose)

Marshmallow, Newberry. Oliver, a middle aged bachelor **dog**, lived in a city apartment. (Cat)

Little Black, a Pony, Farley. I am a little **bullfrog** who wants so much to be big, and do the things a big **bullfrog** can do. (Pony)

Make Way for Ducklings, McCloskey. Mr. and Mrs. Mallard looked for a place to live in **Chicago.** (Boston)

Madeline, Bemelmans. I am the heroine of this story, and live in Paris, France, in an **apartment house.** (Boarding school)

Lonely Veronica, Duvoisin. I was a happy **giraffe** living in the river until men came to build a highway, and took me to a zoo. (Hippopotamus)

In the Forest, Ets. I had a new horn and a paper hat and went to **jog in the park** when I saw a lion, 2 baby elephants, 2 brown bears, a baby kangaroo, a stork, 2 monkeys and a rabbit. (Walk in the forest)

Curious George, Rey. I live with my friend, the man with the **green** hat. (Yellow)

Little Toot, Gramatky. Little toot, the **train**, lived in a busy place. (Tugboat)

Sneakers, Brown. These are 7 stories about a very mischievous **kangaroo.** (Cat)

The Tale of Gloucester, Potter. A tailor becomes ill, and can't make the mayor a waistcoat for his wedding on Christmas Day. Some **kittens** make a most beautiful coat. (Mice)

Little Silk, Ayer. 100 years ago Little Silk, a sweet little **scarecrow**, was made. (Padded doll)

Hugo the Hippo, Baum. Hugo tells why he **trusts grownups** but **does not trust children**. (Trusts children. Doesn't trust grownups)

Clear the Track, Slobodkin. Father was sitting reading the paper; Patty was knitting, and Mike was riding his **skateboard** down the hall. (Bike)

One Fine Day, Hogrogian. A **beaver** walked through the woods, drank milk from a pail of milk, and an old woman chopped off his tail. (Fox)

Will Spring Be Early? Or Will Spring Be Late?, Johnson. A groundhog falsely alarms the animals that spring is here since he sees a **daffodil**. (Plastic red flower)

Harry the Dirty Dog, Zion. Harry was a **black dog** with **white spots**. (White dog with black spots)

Pet Show, Keats. All the kids are on their way to the pet show, but Archie's cat has disappeared, so he brings a **goldfish**. (A germ in a jar)

Mike Mulligan and his Steam Shovel, Burton. Mike's steam shovel's name is **Florence**. (Mary Ann)

Jasmine, Duvoisin. Jasmine is a cow in the farmyard who was different because she wore a **dress**. (Hat)

Crocus, Duvoisin. Crocus is a **canary** who loses his teeth. (Crocodile)

Grades 4–6

Huckleberry Finn, Twain. Together with my friend, Jim, a runaway slave, we float down the **Nile River** on a raft. (Mississippi)

Runaway Ralph, Cleary. Ralph bounced along the mountain highway which he thought made a good road for a **cat**. It was a wild night of adventure. (Mouse)

The Call of the Wild, London. This is the story of Buck, a **young boy** in the Klondi who leads a pack of wolves. (dog)

More About Paddington, Bond. I am an exasperating and endearing **hamster** who lives with the Brown family in London, and my near disasters somehow end triumphally. (Bear)

Twenty Thousand Leagues Under the Sea, Verne. Captain Nemo fights against monsters in the *Nautilus*, a **clipper ship**. (Submarine)

Return from Witch Mountain, Key. This book is a **realistic book** about a power-crazed doctor. (Fantasy)

Strawberry Girl, Lenski. Birdie Boyer and family raise **horses** in Florida, and incite the hostility of their neighbors, the Slators. (Strawberries)

Shadow of a Bull, Wojciechowska. Manolo Olivar was the son of a **farmer** and he was expected to grow up to be just like him. (Bullfighter)

Pinocchio, Collodi. I am a puppet who comes to life, and my **ears** get bigger when I tell a lie. (Nose grows larger)

A Christmas Carol, Dickens. This is a Christmas story, and a story about Scrooge, who was very **generous and kind**. (Stingy and unkind)

Miss Hickory, Bailey. When great-granny Brown moved to Boston, I was faced with spending the severe New Hampshire winter alone. I was a **rag doll**. (A country woman, with the body of an applewood twig and head of a hickory nut)

Ginger Pye, Eleanor Estes. The Pye family is happy until a man with a mustard-colored hat comes, and their **bird**, Ginger, disappears. (Dog)

Rufus M., Estes. Rufus Moffat is the **villain** in a series of adventures. **He does everything wrong.** (Hero. Finds money when his family needs it, etc.)

The Summer of the Swans, Byars. **Sara** became lost in this story. (Charlie, her mentally retarded brother, was lost and then found)

Goodbye Mr. Chips, Hilton. In this book, Mr. Chips is a **public librarian.** (Schoolmaster)

Green Mansions, W.H. Hudson. The setting of this story takes place in the jungles of **East Asia**. (South America)

Ramona, Helen Hunt Jackson. This is a **mystery** of the finest type. (Romance)

Roller Skates, Ruth Sawyer. This story takes place in **1950 in New Mexico.** (1890's in New York)

Highpockets, John R. Tunis. Cecil McDade, or Highpockets to millions of fans, and right fielder for the Dodgers, was a **tremendously popular** character. (Unpopular)

The Witches of Worm, Zilpha K. Snyder. Worm was really a **spider** in this story. (Cat)

The Jargoon Pard, Andre Norton. This story is a **fantasy**. (Science fiction)

The Tough Winter, Robert Lawson. The rabbits in this story live in the **hills of South Carolina.** (Fields and woods of a Connecticut Hill)

The Shadows of Jeremy Pimm, Betsy Haynes. **Neil tried to control Jeremy Pimm** when he suggested ways of dealing with parents who tried to run his life. (Jeremy Pimm tried to control Neil)

Sounder, William Armstrong. Sounder is a **raccoon**. (Coon dog)

Almost Like Sisters, Betty Cavanna. This story takes place in **Ohio**.
(Boston)

57. Irish Folklore and Legend

    C Blarney Stone
    E Cuchulainn
    A Finn MacCool
    B Giant's Causeway
    D Shamrock

A A leader of the Irish warriors of the A.D. 100's or 200's.

B A formation of rock columns

C A person who kisses it will be eloquent

D The national flower of Ireland

E The hero of the Cooley Cattle Raid; Ireland's most famous tale
of ancient time

58. Greek Gods and Goddesses Match

A	AEOLUS		**E**	HYGEIA
R	APHRODITE		**HH**	HYMEN
DD	APOLLO		**JJ**	HYPERION
EE	ARES		**II**	IRIS
NN	ARTEMIS		**V**	MORPHEUS
J	ASCLEPIUS		**D**	MUSES
OO	ATHENA		**BB**	NEMESIS
CC	ATLAS		**Y**	NEREUS
M	BOREAS		**KK**	PAN
P	CALLIOPE		**I**	PERSEPHONE
F	CRONUS		**X**	PLUTUS
PP	DEMETER		**H**	POSEIDON

G	DIONYSUS	FF	PROMETHEUS
T	GRACES	Z	PROTEUS
MM	HADES	GG	RHEA
U	HEBE	AA	SATYR
O	HECATE	C	THANATOS
B	HELIOS	W	TITANS
S	HEPHAESTUS, TEMPLE OF	Q	TRITON
LL	HERA	N	URANUS
K	HERMES	L	ZEUS

HH   God of marriage

II   A golden-winged goddess of the rainbow, and a messenger of the gods

JJ   One of 12 children of gods Uranus and Gaea, members of a race of giant gods

KK   God of the forests and meadows

LL   Queen of the gods who reigned on Mount Olympus by the side of Zeus

MM   God of the underworld

NN   Goddess of childbirth, hunting and the moon

OO   Goddess of warfare and wisdom

PP   Goddess of agriculture and civilized life

A   Father of the winds

B   The first god of the sun

C   God of death

D   Goddesses of the arts and sciences

E   Goddess of health

F   Did not represent a place, function, event of quality

G   God of wine

H   God of sea

I   Goddess of agriculture

J   God of healing

K   A schemer, and the messenger of the gods

L   The king of heaven, god of justice and oaths

M   God of the storm and winds

N   The oldest god: gave light, heat and rain to earth

O   Goddess of ghosts

P   The muse of epic poetry

Q   A sea god; he stirred up or calmed waves

R   Goddess of love and beauty

S   A Greek temple for the god of fire

T   The 3 daughters of Zeus and Eurynome: They were the goddesses of the talents of music and arts

U   Goddess of youth

V   God of dreams

W   An ancient race of gods

X   God of wealth

Y   Old man of the sea

Z A herdsman for flocks of seals and creatures of the sea

AA Gods of the woods: part human and part goat or horse

BB Goddess of vengeance

CC One of the Titans who supported the heavens on his shoulders

DD God of light, purity, and the sun

EE God of war

FF A Titan, stole fire from gods and gave it to man

GG Goddess of the growth of natural things

59. Egyptian Mythology Match

A	AMON	**G**	OSIRIS
B	ANUBIS	**H**	RE
C	APIS	**I**	SERAPIS
D	HATHOR	**J**	SET
E	HORUS	**K**	SPHINX
F	ISIS	**L**	THEBES
	M	THOTH		

G Main god of the underworld

K An imaginary creature with the head of a man; body, legs, feet and tail of a lion. Guards temples and tombs

D Goddess of heaven, joy, music and love. Represented by a cow

A Chief god of ancient Egyptians. Represented by a human with a headdress and two big feathers

I God of healing; protector of sailors

M God of learning, letters and wisdom

E   God of light and heaven

B   God of the underworld. Represented by a crouching dog or jackal

L   The Greek name of a city in ancient Egypt that was capital for Egyptian kings.

J   God of evil. Represented with a head — a cross between a donkey and a pig.

C   Sacred bull

H   God of the sun; god of the living

F   Mother of all things, of all the elements, origin of all time. Represented by a human with crown

60. German Folklore and Legend Match

A	BRUNHILD	**G**	NIBELUNG
B	FAUST	**H**	NIBELUNGENLIED
C	LORELEI	**I**	NIX
D	MEPHISTOPHELES	**J**	PIED PIPER OF HAMELIN
E	MOUSE TOWER	**K**	SIEGFRIED
F	MUNCHAUSEN, BARON	**L**	TANNHAUSER

H   A german epic poem

D   The Devil

B A magician who said he was in league with the Devil

L A German minstrel

J Got rid of all the rats and children of Hamelin

C A high cliff above the Rhine River in Germany. Echo heard there can lure boats to destruction

A A mythical heroine

E A tower on a small island in the Rhine River. Bishop Hatto went there to escape an army of mice

K A hero of many German legends

F The central character and the narrator in an anonymous booklet of tall tales

G The children of the mist; a group of dwarfs

I A water sprite or little people with golden hair and green teeth

61. Folklore and Legends of Other Lands Match

A	AESOP'S FABLES	**K**	EPIC OF GILGAMESH
B	ALADDIN	**L**	ROLAND
C	AMADIS OF GAUL	**M**	SANTA CLAUS
D	ARABIAN NIGHTS	**N**	SCHEHERAZADE
E	BERSERKER	**O**	SEVEN SLEEPERS OF EPHESUS
F	EL CID	**P**	WILLIAM TELL
G	CINDERELLA	**Q**	TUBAL-CAIN
H	DON JUAN	**R**	WEREWOLF
I	FLYING DUTCHMAN	**S**	ARNOLD VON WINKELRIED
J	FOUNTAIN OF YOUTH		

D   200 stories

L   Hero of the French epic poem

R   A man-wolf

A   Animal stories that illustrate human faults and virtues

H   A handsome nobleman

N   Legendary Queen who told the stories in the Arabian Nights

P   A legendary hero of Switzerland

F   One of Spain's national heroes; real name was Rodrigo Diaz

B   Hero in the Arabian Nights

M   A legendary old man who brings gifts to children

Q   A metal smith of olden times

C   Spanish romance of chivalry

G   A beautiful, but shabbily treated heroine

J   An imaginary spring

E   Hero in Norse folklore; he needed no armor when he fought

I   A legendary ship

K   One of the oldest epics in world literature

S   A legendary national hero of Switzerland; Battle of Sempach

O   Christian youths in old legend who escaped persecution by Emperor Decius

62. British Folklore and Legend Match

A	ALLAN-A-DALE	**M**	KING-HORN
B	BARBARA ALLEN	**N**	SIR LANCELOT
C	KING ARTHUR	**O**	SIR LAUNFAL
D	BEOWULF	**P**	LITTLE JOHN
E	ROBERT BRUCE	**Q**	PETER PAN
F	EXCALIBUR	**R**	PUCK
G	FRIAR TUCK	**S**	ROB ROY
H	SIR GALAHAD	**T**	ROBIN HOOD
I	LADY GODIVA	**U**	ROUND TABLE
J	GUY OF WARWICK	**V**	DICK TURPIN
K	HAVELOK THE DANE	**W**	DICK WHITTINGTON
L	HOLY GRAIL		

R A mischievous spirit or elf who tormented people in jest

W An English merchant

G A legendary character who could defeat Little John and Robin Hood as an archer

P One of Robin Hood's troupe who was over 7 feet tall

A Joined Robin Hood's band when his sweetheart was forced to marry an old knight

D An epic poem in Old English

L The cup Jesus used at the Last Supper

T A legendary hero of the common folk

O A knight of King Arthur's Round Table

I Her husband agreed to reduce the taxes if she would ride naked through the town

C A legendary king of medieval England

B She's called bonny and hardhearted

Q A boy who refuses to grow up

M The most crucial character in the first English romance

V An English robber

S A Scottish outlaw

U A famous table in the legends of King Arthur; Merlin made it

K A hero of several English stories; became King of Denmark

E A Scottish king who tried to free his country from English rule

H The most virtuous and noble knight of King Arthur's Round Table

N A British knight in times of King Arthur's Round Table; famous for skill and bravery in combat

J Rescued England from Danish rule

F The sword of King Arthur

63. Hindu Myth Match

A	BRAHMAN	**F**	THUG
B	MAHABHARATA	**G**	VEDAS
C	MANU	**H**	VISHNU
D	RAMAYANA	**I**	JUGGERNAUT
E	SHIVA	**J**	BHAGAVAD-GITA

A   The Supreme World-Spirit

H   The World-Preserver

D   An epic poem in India — partly historical and partly legendary

J   Sacred writing discussing the meaning and nature of Existence

I   Famous Hindu temple and idol

B   An epic poem in India; an adventure and religious tale

G   The oldest sacred books of India

C   The ancestor of the human race

F   Members of an old society in India who killed in the name of religion

E   The second God in the triad of Brahma, Siva, and Vishnu

64. American Folklore and Legend Match

A	ALDEN FAMILY	N	JOHN HENRY
B	JOHNNY APPLESEED	O	HIAWATHA
C	SAM BASS	P	JOHNNY INKSLINGER
D	BILLY THE KID	Q	JESSE JAMES
E	DANIEL BOONE	R	WILLIAM KIDD
F	BUFFALO BILL	S	JEAN LAFFITE
G	PAUL BUNYAN	T	JOE MAGARAC
H	KIT CARSON	U	SNAKE MAGEE
I	DAVID CROCKETT	V	MINNEHAHA
J	EVANGELINE	W	PECOS BILL
K	FEBOLD FEBOLDSON	X	POCAHONTAS
L	MIKE FINK	Y	RIP VAN WINKLE
M	BARBARA FRIETCHIE		

K Legendary tall tale hero of Nebraska; humerous exaggerations

S A pirate from France

V An Indian maiden in Henry Wadsworth Longfellow's poem

X Captain John Smith said she saved his life

J First long narrative poem by Longfellow

G Legendary hero of the lumberjacks

A Colonial family who came to America on the Mayflower

O An Indian hero of Henry Wadsworth Longfellow's poem

L Won fame as an expert shot; a frontiersman and boatman

W Mythical super-cowboy and inventor of roping

Y Slept for 20 years

U Legendary oil-well driller

H Hero of the American West; a fur trapper, scout, Indian fighter and soldier

C A Texas Robin Hood

F William Frederick Cody; a showman and a frontiersman

Q A notorious outlaw

T A 7-foot giant; mythical strong man of steel

R A famous pirate from Scotland

N A legendary Black steel-driver

D A killer and cattle thief in New Mexico

I Frontiersman who told tall tales

E Most well-known colonial pioneer

M The heroine of John Greenleaf Whittier's poem

B John Chapman: legendary figure, herb doctor, nurseryman, military hero, and religious enthusiast

P Paul Bunyan's timekeeper

65. Match Author to Famous Quotation

A	SIR WALTER SCOTT	**N**	CHARLES DICKENS
B	MENANDER	**O**	ALEXANDER POPE
C	RUPERT BROOKE	**P**	ABRAHAM LINCOLN
D	ALFRED LORD TENNYSON	**Q**	ALGERNON CHARLES
E	WILLIAM CONGREVE		SWINBURNE
F	WILLIAM SHAKESPEARE	**R**	SIR WINSTON CHURCHILL
G	ROBERT BROWNING	**S**	MIGUEL DE CERVANTES
H	WILLIAM WORDSWORTH		SAAVEDRA
I	ERNEST DOWSON	**T**	OVID
J	THOMAS GRAY	**U**	ROBERT BURNS
K	OSCAR WILDE	**V**	JONATHAN SWIFT
L	FRANCIS BACON	**W**	HERMAN MELVILLE
M	SAMUEL TAYLOR COLERIDGE	**X**	HENRY DAVID THOREAU

D "Knowledge comes, but wisdom lingers."

K "Conscience makes egotists of us all."

Q "Be silent always when you doubt your sense."

F "For Brutus is an honorable man."

X "The mass of men lead lives of quiet desperation."

W "A whale ship was my Yale College and my Harvard."

N "What a world of gammon and spinnage it is."

S "The worm will turn."

C "We have come into our heritage."

E "Retired to their tea and scandal."

T "The most potent thing in life is habit."

M "For he on honey — dew hath fed and drunk the milk of paradise."

R "I have nothing to offer but blood, toil, tears, and sweat."

T "Gone with the wind."

Q "Blossom by blossom the spring begins."

A "Blood's thicker than water."

H "The light that never was, on sea or land."

U "The light that led astray was light from Heaven."

F "To thine own self be true."

L "Virtue is like a rich stone, best plain set."

V "The sight of you is good for sore eyes."

P "Government of the people, by the people, and for the people."

B "Call a spade a spade."

J "A favorite has no friend."

G "Faultless to a fault."

66. Scrambled Contest

The following scrambled or jumbled words are titles of books.

Grades 3–6

DONEURS *Sounder*
HOCINIOPC *Pinocchio*
TE'SCHOTARL BEW *Charlotte's Web*
TARUTS TILTEL *Stuart Little*
A MITSACSHR RACLO *A Christmas Carol*
AMEJS NAD HET NAGIT HAPCE *James and the Giant Peach*
RIELAHC DAN EHT LOCHCOEAT TAFCYOR *Charlie and the Chocolate Factory*
NICATTASF R.M OXF *Fantastic Mr. Fox*
HERSPIWAT WNDO *Watership Down*
GEGRIN YEP *Ginger Pye*
UFURS M. *Rufus M.*
HET DUNDERH SSREEDS *The Hundred Dresses*
HTE HGTSO FO DINYW LILH *The Ghost of Windy Hill*
DADECI WODWONAL *Caddie Woodlawn*
NAEJ REEY *Jane Eyre*
KCSOS *Socks*
HTE LEEHW NO HTE HOSCOL *The Wheel on the School*
HTE TENYWT-NEO LAOBONLS *The Twenty-one Balloons*
SAHN KINREBR *Hans Brinker*
SIMYT FO GEATEUNHOCIC *Misty of Chincoteague*
DOL LEELYR *Old Yeller*
LORREL KESATS *Roller Skates*
BOYM CIDK *Moby Dick*
SEERTAUR DISNAL *Treasure Island*
KFAYRE DIRAFY *Freaky Friday*

Grades 1–3

TUNEIAP *Petunia*
NEROVAIC *Veronica*
RUSCOC *Crocus*

MASIJEN *Jasmine*
HTE LEAT FO TEPRE BABRIT *The Tale of Peter Rabbit*
GANUS DAN HTE ATC *Angus and the Cat*
HTE TILTLE LISDAN *The Little Island*
RAMHSLAMLOW *Marshmallow*
LEGGOGS *Goggles*
IH TCA *Hi, Cat*
HTE NSOYW ADY *The Snowy Day*
NEJIE'SN TAH *Jennie's Hat*
LIMNIOLS FO TACS *Millions of Cats*
HTE TTIELL USEOH *The Little House*
LEDINAME *Madeline*
ABARB HTE GINK *Babar the King*
TILLET OTOT *Little Toot*
POOLY *Loopy*
ROUUCIS REGEOG *Curious George*
NEO NIEF YAD *One Fine Day*
HTE TAC NI HTE TAH *The Cat in the Hat*
MIET FO DONERW *Time of Wonder*
CILULEL *Lucille*
HTE TOSMR KOOB *The Storm Book*
LIM'SLAIW LODL *William's Doll*

67. Genre Match

This may be used as a ditto contest, with all the categories —
Mystery, Fantasy, Science Fiction, Historical Fiction and Humor —
printed at the top.

The Borrowers (Norton) FANTASY
Ramona the Brave (Cleary) HUMOR
"Encyclopedia Brown" books (Sobol) MYSTERY
Island of One (Bunting) SCIENCE FICTION
Little House in the Big Woods (Wilder) HISTORICAL FICTION
Poor Stainless (Norton) FANTASY
Henry Huggins (Cleary) HUMOR
Mrs. Piggle-Wiggle (MacDonald) HUMOR
"Alfred Hitchcock" books MYSTERY
Caddie Woodlawn (Brink) HISTORICAL FICTION

Buzzbugs (Carter) SCIENCE FICTION
Pippi Longstocking (Lindgren) HUMOR
"McBroom" books (Fleischman) HUMOR
The High King (Alexander) FANTASY
Socks (Cleary) HUMOR
Freaky Friday (Rodgers) FANTASY
Adam of the Road (Gray) HISTORICAL FICTION
My Robot Buddy (Slote) SCIENCE FICTION
Flaming arrows (Steele) HISTORICAL FICTION
"Trixie Belden" books (Kenny) MYSTERY
"Miss Pickerell" books (MacGregor) SCIENCE FICTION
"Danny Dunn" books (Williams) SCIENCE FICTION
Henry Reed's Baby-sitting Service (Roberston) HUMOR
Mary Poppins (Travers) FANTASY
My Brother Sam is Dead (Collier) HISTORICAL

68. Authors — Can You Guess Who?

What a flower does when it matures BLUME
Fire does what BURNS
This guy's not short LONGFELLOW
This is the life of RILEY
What the hunted animal must do when he gets shot at with an arrow
    SHAKESPEARE
A dreary color GRAY
Getting into mischief will cause one to get the DICKENS
An animal; a symbol of peace LAMB
Not tamer, but WILDER
A foggy mist HAYS
The small girl said it after eating potato chips MOORE
A western European country FRANCE
The Yale song BULLA
A state that begins with New YORK
A fort in New Jersey DIXON
We build with it and burn it WOOD
Oposite of black WHITE

Not old, but YOUNG
To catch a whale SPEARE
Capital of England LONDON
Not despair, but HOPE
To search for HUNT
To unlock it, you need the KEY
Opposite of blurry CLEARY
You'll get the dickens; you'll hear plenty of FLACK

69. Folk Tale and Nation Match

The Cat and the Devil FRANCE
One Fine Day ARMENIA
Tops and Bottoms GREAT BRITAIN
The Three Gold Pieces GREECE
Princess of the Full Moon AFRICA
East of the Sun and West of the Moon NORWAY
The Dancing Kettle JAPAN
Turnabout NORWAY
Ghosts Go Haunting SCOTLAND
The Rescue of the Sun ESKIMO — UNITED STATES
Sixty at a Blow TURKEY
Peter and the Wolf RUSSIA
Which Was Witch KOREA
The Baker and the Basilisk AUSTRIA
The Piece of Fire HAITI
Urashima Taro and the Princess of the Sea JAPAN
Jorinda and Jorinquel GERMANY
Once the Mullah PERSIA
Why Mosquitoes Buzz in Peoples Ears AFRICA
Pecos Bill UNITED STATES
Jataka Tales INDIA
Good Sense and Good Fortune POLAND
Hansel and Gretel GERMANY
Puss in Boots FRANCE
The Wizard and His Magic Powder CHANNEL ISLANDS
The Bremen Town Musicians GERMANY
The Story of Prince Ivan, the Firebird and the Gray Wolf RUSSIA
Clever Manka CZECHOSLOVAKIA

The Mouse-Princess FRANCE
Johnny-Cake ENGLAND
The Cock, the Mouse, and the Little Red Hen ENGLAND
Beauty and the Beast FRANCE
The Frog Prince GERMANY
The Three Sneezes SWITZERLAND
The Most Precious Possession ITALY
Lion Outwitted by Hare AFRICA
The Jokes of Single-Toe SPAIN
King O'Toole and His Goose IRELAND
Three Billy Goats Gruff NORWAY
Joco and the Fishbone ARABIA
Hidden Laiva FINLAND
High, Wide and Handsome BURMA
The Cat and the Mouse SPAIN
Snow White and the Seven Dwarfs GERMANY
King Bartek POLAND
The Fireflies CZECHOSLOVAKIA
The Grindstone of God; a Fable SIBERIA
Troll Weather NORWAY
My Mother Is the Most Beautiful Woman in the World RUSSIA
Tino and the Typhoon PHILIPPINE ISLANDS

70. Authors Rhyme

Another class activity, or may be used as a bulletin board project. The librarian lists words that rhyme with an author's name; the students must write the authors' names.

Moose	SEUSS	Bets	MARIE HALL ETS
Given	TODD RUTHVEN	Yield	RACHEL FIELD
Vermont	MARC SIMONT	May stood	CAROLYN HAYWOOD
Tone	PELAGIE DOANE	Sack	MARJORIE FLACK
Meats	JACK EZRA KEATS	Bird	CLEMENT HURD
Bunt	IRENE HUNT	Clear	EDWARD LEAR
Liars	BETSY BYARS	Beef	MUNRO LEAF
Whacks	MARILYN SACHS	Awesome	ROBERT LAWSON
Luck	PEARL BUCK	Baloney	LEO LIONNI
Noun	MARGARET WISE BROWN	Nobel	ARNOLD LOBEL

Lock   EMMA LILLIAN BROCK   Leeks   ESTHER MEEKS
Link   CAROL RYRIE BRINK   Legs   CORNELIA MEIGS
Marina   BETTINA   Beans   FLORENCE MEANS
Certain   VIRGINIA LEE BURTON   Poor   LILLIAN MOORE
Misty   AGATHA CHRISTIE   Blueberry   CLARE NEWBERRY
Mark   ANN NOLAN CLARK   Horton   HELEN FULLER ORTON
Leery   BEVERLY CLEARY   Calmer   HELEN PALMER
Lemons   SAMUEL CLEMENS   Mall   GRACE PAULL
Book   OLIVE COOK   Blotter   BEATRIX POTTER
Belong   MEINDERT DE JONG   Land   PAUL AND ANN RAND
Podge   MARY DODGE   Bay   HANS AUGUSTO REY
Beggar   EDWARD EAGER   Bounds   GLEN ROUNDS
Beer   ELIZABETH GEORGE SPEARE Bolts   MARY STOLZ

71. Newbery Award Winner Match

Place on the bulletin board book jackets of a number of Newbery Award-winning books with mixed-up index cards of their summaries. Have students in the class place the correct index card beneath the book jacket.

72. Find the Titles

Here is a *story, a story* of *Parsley, Petunia, lonely Veronica, Periwinkle* and *Crocus*, and of *why mosquitoes buzz in people's ears*. It's a tale of *the mighty hunter in the forest, a fish out of water* and *Harry and the lady next door*. You might say that this is the story of *mouse tales*, of *mixed-up magic* and *having fun one fine day* and during *the quiet evening*.

Well, *tell me some more*. This is a tale of all of the books that *Miss Terry at the library* keeps on the shelves. *May I visit where the wild things are* and *Mr. Fong's toy shop* during *the first day of school? No funny business* now. *How far will a rubber band stretch? What's that noise? Stop, stop*. You must have gotten up on *the wrong side of the bed* this morning. *Who's a pest? Do you hear what I hear? Quiet! There's a canary in the library*. You can also hear the *song of the swallows, a klippity klop, the brook*, and *what did the rock say?*

Who lives there? Our fur and feathered friends; Flicka Ricka Dicka and the girl next door; the girl who loved the wind; drummer Hoff; Leopold the see-through crumbpicker; Dandelion; Mr. Messy; Anansi the spider; Taro and the bamboo shoot; Sam, Bangs, and moonshine; three poor tailors; Andy and the lion; and *lonely Maria;* and *the king who could not sleep.*

What's happening there? *Dreams* and *curious George learns the alphabet* and *it's where the wild apples grow. Do you know what I know? A tree is nice; everything about Easter rabbits; I saw a ship a sailing. What do you want to be? Nothing at all.* I'm hungry! *Truffles for lunch. Stone soup* and *three stalks of corn. Watch out for the chicken feet in your soup.*

Will I have a friend? Of course, you can be *little bear's friend. A friend is someone who likes you. Wait till Sunday* to find *Petunia's treasure.* Then we will take the *quito express* over in the *meadow* and cuddle up *in a pumpkin shell* with our *goggles* to read about *one morning in Maine.* Then we'll take the *little toot on the thames* back to *the calico jungle. When is tomorrow?* I can't wait to come back here. The library is truly *my castle.*

73. Fairy Tale Telegram

Each letter in "Fairy Tales" suggests tales from all over the world.

F FREDERICK ... FISHERMAN & HIS WIFE ... FROG PRINCE ... FIVE PEAS IN A POD ... FORTUNATA
A ASPENDOG
I IVAN THE FOOL ... IRON-HEADED MAN
R RUMPELSTILTSKIN ... RAPUNZEL ... ROSE RED
Y YULETIDE SPECTERS ... YELLOW DWARF ... (THE) YOUTH WHO WAS TO SERVE THREE YEARS WITHOUT PAY
T TOM THUMB ... TWELVE DANCING PRINCESSES ... THUMBLING THE GIANT, THUMBLING THE DWARF ... THUMBELINA ... TINTELLE'S MOTHER
A (THE) ANIMAL FAIRIES ... ALI BABA
L LAZY HARRY ... LEAN LISA ... LITTLE RED RIDING HOOD
E ELVES AND THE SHOEMAKER ... ENCHANTED RING
S SNOW WHITE ... SIX SOLDIERS OF FORTUNE ... SLEEPING BEAUTY

74. Foxes

A diagram of a naturalist and a ring of fox dens is made for the bulletin board as shown below. In each den is a category of books: fiction book or picture book according to the grade level of the class. Or else, this activity could be used on an individual basis. Each den may contain a specific category or type of book: for example, mystery; science fiction; historical fiction; biography. As each den is approached, the student must read the specific category listed, and choose a book from the library. Upon finishing the book, the student presents an index card summary to the librarian to indicate that the book was read. The librarian then gives the student a fox, and the student goes on to the next den. When all eight dens have been trailed, and books read, students are honored by placing a list of the student names who have read eight books in a specified period of time, for example, six weeks. The student who reaches all the dens, and completes the books before anyone else, gets special recognition.

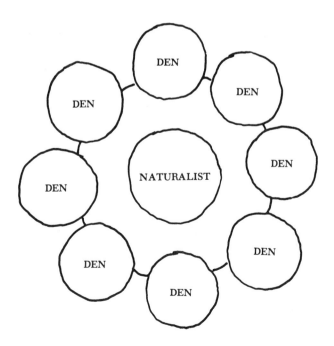

75. Taxi

A taxi route is either outlined on the bulletin board, or the game is conducted on an individual basis. The diagram below is provided for students. Three streets are made from categories of books lined in a row with the specific categories serving as houses. The taxi garage is placed in the upper left-hand corner of the chart where the taxi is emerging. The librarian calls the taxi to drive to, say, an animal story with each student taking such a book to read. The pupil draws a line from the garage to the house where the librarian tells the taxi to go. Then the next house is called where the taxi must drive. Crossing a previous line disqualifies the student to continue the activity. Each house visited, or category of book must be read before continuing on to the next house. The winner of the exercise reaches the end destination by completing the books, and without crossing any lines.

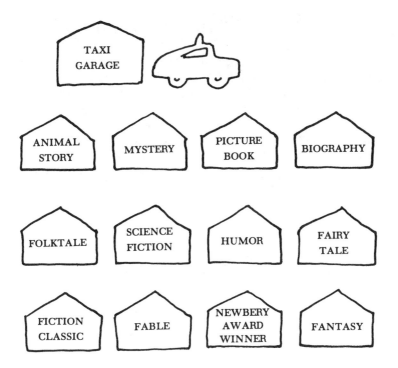

76. Travel to Foreign Lands

This activity includes non-fiction books and/or fiction books with foreign settings. A world map can be mounted on the wall or bulletin board with colored pin heads attached to small passports with the student's name written on it. The student who has visited the most foreign countries wins a travel poster (from a travel agent). Or else the student who has traveled the furthest distance from his own home state may be chosen as the winner of this contest.

77. Teacher's Hobby

Books on hobbies are displayed, and a list of the hobbies of all the teachers of the school is posted. The student who correctly identifies the hobby of each teacher is the winner of the contest.

78. Walking the Plank

A bulletin board is created for this contest. Each teacher's name is written (i.e. "Mrs. Jensen's class" or "Mr. Smith's class") on a construction paper marker. A ship is drawn on the bulletin board with a plank. As each class visits the library, the class marker is placed on the plank. Each group is given an assignment with reference books, and students must correctly answer the reference question they receive. If the entire class, or each group of students completes the task correctly, the class is saved from being thrown in the sea. If, however, one group does not complete the task given, or completes it incorrectly, the entire class must "walk the plank," and is dumped into the sea.

79. Wall Hanging Mystery

A bulletin board gives clues of where to look in the library for a specific book or answer to a question. Whoever solves the mystery wins a "Sherlock Holmes" Award.

80. Track and Field Events

This activity for the bulletin board may include throwing the discus; running the high jump; javelin throw; standing broad jump; cross-country run; hurdle races; sprinting (dashes); and track-relay races. List a number of categories that have to be read such as: a horse story; a cat story; a biography; a fairy tale; or a book on one of the states. Once these obstacles have been read, or gotten over, the event is finished. The winner is the first person to cross the finish line, or to throw the discus the farthest, or jump the highest in the high jump.

81. Tug of War

Two classes may have a tug-of-war. Both ends of a rope or cord are tacked to the bulletin board. Paper books depicting books read by each class are placed on each side of the middle line. The class who reads the most books (say in three weeks time) wins the tug-of-war. The student must present to the teacher or librarian an index card summary or other indication that the book was read completely.

82. Mouse Cage

Students read a mouse story. Each time a book is completed, the student is given a paper mouse to place in a giant mouse cage. The mouse announces the student's name and title of book. Whoever reads the most mice stories, or catches the most mice wins.

Grades 1–3

Mouse Days: A Book of Seasons (Lionni)
Greentail Mouse (Lionni)
Frederick (Lionni)
Geraldine, the Music Mouse (Lionni)
Alexander and the Wind-up Mouse (Lionni)
Anatole (Titus)

The Mouses' Terrible Halloween (Kelley)
The Story of Miss Moppet (Potter)
Home: The Tale of a Mouse (Schlein)
The Guard Mouse (Freeman)
Snippy and Snappy (Gag)
The King, the Mice and the Cheese (Gurney)
The Old Stump (Hawkinson)
Baseball Mouse (Hoff)
Sylvester, the Mouse with the Musical Ear (Holl)
Mouse Tales (Lobel)
The Tale of Johnny Town-mouse (Potter)
Ten in a Family (Steiner)
Henry (Vreeken)
Noisy Nora (Wells)
Mousekin's Christmas Eve (Miller)
Mousekin's Family (Miller)
Mice on Ice (Yolen)
Mice Twice (Low)
Mice Came in Early This Year (Lapp)

Grades 4–6

The Mouse and the Motorcycle (Cleary)
Abel's Island (Steig)
Stuart Little (White)
Runaway Ralph (Cleary)
I Am a Mouse (Coggins)
Walter the Lazy Mouse (Flack)
Ben and Me; a New and Astonishing Life of Benjamin Franklin as Written by His Good Mouse Amos; Lately Discovered (Lawson)
Basil of Baker Street (Titus)
Jeremy Mouse Book (Scarry)
Adventures of Danny Meadow Mouse (Burgess)

83. Animal Character Designs

For a display, students may outline animal designs using the name of the animal character.

84. Crosswords

Across

1. Petunia is a ...

2. *Little Toot* is a ...
3. Who changed Willy, the wind-up mouse into a regular mouse in Lionni's *Alexander and the Wind-up Mouse?*

4. Loopy is a ...

5. What did Mary Ann, the steam shovel become at the end of the book, *Mike Mulligan and His Steam Shovel?*

6. Veronica is a ...
7. Parsley is a ...

8. The name of Mike Mulligan's steam shovel ...

Down

1. Angus is a ...

2. Who is Babar?

3. Pippa is a ...

4. How many hats did Bartholomew Cubbins take off?

5. Periwinkle is a ...

6. Snippy and Snappy are ...

7. Name of Lionni's bird with the golden wings ...

8. Last name of Bartholomew in the Dr. Seuss book ...

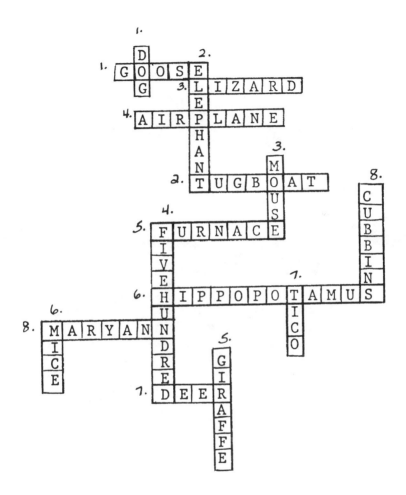

Part III
Active Participation

85. Olympics

This activity may include any sport such as volleyball; toss-ball; croquet; tennis; soccer; football; archery; or bowling. Students participate in this activity either as a bulletin board game or as an active question game. For example, the class is divided into two teams for volleyball. A question is asked of the first team, and if they answer it correctly, they are allowed to hit the ball over to the second team. If they do not answer correctly, then the opposing team gains a point. Or as a bulletin board game, two or more classes compete for points. Points may be gained by the reading of books. Certain types of books such as historical fiction, mystery, or science fiction are assigned more points than are picture books. For instance, picture books may be allotted one point, while historical fiction is granted 10 points. The class that gains the most points at the end of the one month olympics is the winner. Classes may participate in any or all of the events.

86. Jungle Book Jubilee

An exhibit of non-fiction animal books are selected with an array of wild animal books included. Each student in a class selects one book to take out and read. Fiction animal stories may be placed with the non-fiction books. Upon coming to the library, students may state three interesting facts which were learned while reading a book. If they selected a fiction animal story, they could tell the class a brief summary of it.

87. Paperback Book Exchange

A paperback book exchange may be set up with paperback novels brought in by students. Students may sign their names to a sheet of paper indicating that they have taken a book. Or other books — discards or gifts — may be used for such a book exchange. This should be with the supervision and approval of the librarian.

88. Author's Birthday

A big box is decorated as a birthday present. Inside are little gifts (e.g. pencils, erasers, colored pencils, paints, stickers). Posted nearby each month are the names of authors and illustrators who celebrate a birthday. A bit of information is also given about each particular author or illustrator, and samples of their books are exhibited nearby for examination. Upon reading one of the books, the student may fill out a 3 x 5 card or a questionnaire, briefly reporting on the book. After doing this, the student may take a present out of the giant birthday present box. This activity encourages reading and fosters an awareness of authors and illustrators.

89. Medieval Revelry

Stories of long ago may be featured as a topic of interest in the library. Books pertaining to castles, knights, the Crusades, gothic art, tournaments, clothing, shelter, and other related subjects may be displayed. Special models could be made by students. Students may dress in medieval costumes on the day they are to take part in the revelry. Medieval music may be played for background. The librarian can select fragments of interesting information concerning the period while presenting pictures of the times. The students may bring any information or pictures which they can find to the revelry session to add to the discussion.

90. Laura Ingalls Wilder Celebration

Arrange to honor the books of Laura Ingalls Wilder by displaying a number of them in a display case in the hallway. A special reading of one of these could be done in parts in the library. Displays of models of a prairie scene and covered wagon could be made.

91. Library Posters and Riddles

A best poster contest could be held at the beginning of the school year. Students design their own posters that speak of proper library behavior: having clean hands; protecting books in plastic bags when it rains; keeping pets and small children away from books by placing books on a high shelf; putting books back in their proper places on the shelf in the library; and other library rules and behavior. The librarian or a student poll could decide the winner.

92. Literary Jingles

A contest for the best book jingle is always fun. Students read a novel, and must then write a two to four line jingle that says something appropriate about the novel read. These may be displayed in the library, or else in an exhibit area in the hallway, or an outside bulletin board. The librarian may judge the winner, or a vote could be taken by the students of the school.

93. My Diary

Students may keep a diary made out of construction paper or oak tag. An account of books read, and the type of books (fiction or non-fiction broken down into categories), may be kept. At the end of a semester, they may be displayed in order to spark an interest in the books.

94. Newbery Award Rebus

Newbery Award winning titles may excite potential readers when presented by a rebus. A bulletin board may display the following titles with pictures from old magazines used to substitute for a portion of the title. The capitalized portion of the following winners is a picture with the rest of the title printed on a bulletin board. The students may guess what the book is on an individual basis.

Story of **MAN**kind.
Dark fri**GATE**
TAILS from **SILVER** lands
Shen of the **SEA**
Gay **NECK**
Hit **TEA** her 1st 100 **CALENDAR**   *(Hitty Her First 100 Years)*
CAT who went to heaven
WATERless **MOUNTAIN**
INNvincible lou**EZ**a
White **STAG**
Call it cour**AGED PERSON**   *(Call It Courage)*
MATCH LOCK GUN

Adam of the **ROAD**
Johnny **TREE**main
Miss **HICKORY NUT**
KING of the **WIND**
Amos Fortune, free **MAN**
GINGER PIE   *(Ginger Pye)*
And now me**GULL**   *(And Now Miguel)*
Carry on, Mr. **BOW DITCH**
MIRRORacles on **MAPLE HILL**
RIFLES for Waitie
WITCH of **BLACKBIRD POND**
ONION John
Bronze **BOW**
It's like this, **CAT**
EYE, **WAND** d Pareja
Up a **ROAD** slowly
From the mixed-up **FILES** of Mrs. **BASIL E.** Frank**WHY**ler
   (...Frankweiler)

High **KING**
SUMMER of the **SWANS**
Mrs. **FRISBY** and the **RATS** of **NIMH**
JEWEL E of the **WOLVES**
Slave **DANCER**
M. **SEA** Higgins
Grey **KING**
BRIDGE to Terabithia

95. Famous Last Lines

Same as "Table of Contents" (No. 32) except that the last few lines of the fiction book are used. May also be used orally with a class.

96. Famous First Lines

Same as "Table of Contents" and "Famous Last Lines" except that the first few lines are used. I also use this one orally with a class.

97. Recognition

I use this with my scheduled classes coming to the library. They guess what famous book character, fairy or folk tale character, or historical person these objects or places call to mind.

Grades 1–3

A glass slipper CINDERELLA
An apple WILLIAM TELL
A silver lamp ALADDIN
A wolf RED RIDING HOOD
A steam shovel MIKE MULLIGAN
Blaze BILLY
A lost dog BEPPOLINO (Bettina)
Quito Express PEDRO
Porky COWBOY SAM *(Cowboy Sam and Porky)*

A vegetable garden MR. MCGREGOR
Microscope GREG
Tricycle in the hall MIKE *(Clear the Track)*
A white duck; a white sheep, or Madelon; Patapon JEANNE-MARIE
A germ in a jar ARCHIE *(Pet Show)*
A dog called Kitty THE STUPIDS
A boarding school in Paris MADELINE
Millions of cats A VERY OLD MAN & A VERY OLD WOMAN
A deep, dark forest, or a witch HANSEL AND GRETEL
A new horn and paper hat A LITTLE BOY *(In the Forest)*
Curious George MAN WITH THE YELLOW HAT
Gingerbread Man AN OLD MAN & OLD WOMAN
A long blonde braid RAPUNZEL
A poisonous apple SNOW WHITE
A spinning wheel RUMPELSTILTSKIN
A spindle ROSAMOND — THE SLEEPING BEAUTY
A toy shop MR. FONG
A Maine harbor SALLY
Quakers OBADIAH
A hat JENNIE
Puppets LOUIE
Whistling WILLIE
A snowy day PETER
Chair PETER
A letter AMY
Goggles PETER AND ARCHIE
Crumbpicker LEOPOLD-MINERVA
A drum DRUMMER HOFF
The poppy seeds PABLO
A lost first tooth SALLY *(One Morning in Maine)*
A garden MISS JASTER'S
A poor man with an animal family MISTER PENNY
Swallows coming back JUAN *(Song of the Swallows)*
A little dog, Moustachio MONSIEUR JAMBON
A thorn in a lion's paw ANDY
Pirates MAGGIE
A hammer and the railroad JOHN HENRY
The bad hat and Miss Clavel MADELINE
Hand-me-down clothes MATILDA
Chinese merchant; ships FU

Grades 4-6

Hatchet GEORGE WASHINGTON
Kite BENJAMIN FRANKLIN
A lonely island ROBINSON CRUSOE
A fawn JODY BAXTER *(The Yearling)*
Raft HUCKLEBERRY FINN
Mississippi River HUCKLEBERRY FINN & TOM SAWYER
Lilliputians — under 6" tall; Brobdingnagians — over 6' tall GULLI-
VER
Nautilus CAPTAIN NEMO
Strawberries BIRDIE BOYER
Bullfights MANOLO OLIVAR
A growing nose PINOCCHIO
Christmas dinner SCROOGE
The 21 balloons PROFESSOR WILLIAM WATERMAN SHERMAN
Julie MIYAX
Ginger THE PYE FAMILY
Swans SARA *(The Summer of the Swans)*
A long blond braid RAPUNZEL
A poisonous apple SNOW WHITE
A spinning wheel RUMPELSTILTSKIN
A spindle ROSAMOND — THE SLEEPING BEAUTY
A giant peach JAMES HENRY TROTTER
A candy plant MR. WILLY WONKA
Sherwood Forest ROBIN HOOD
A clue; Mr. Watson SHERLOCK HOLMES
Ultrasonic speech TIA AND TONY
A white whale CAPTAIN AHAB
A miniature world THE BORROWERS
A babysitting service HENRY REED
A cricket in Times Square MARIO BELLINIS
Swiss Alps HEIDI
A hot air balloon MR. PHILEAS FOGG
The prairie and a covered wagon PA, MA, MARY, LAURA & BABY
CARRIE
Post-war Germany; two freezing rooms LECHOWS *(The Ark)*
13th century England ROBIN *(The Door in the Wall)*
Ribsy, the dog HENRY AND BEEZUS
A mother who dies GROVER

A hilarious pheasant-snatching expedition DANNY *(Danny the Champion of the World)*

Life in 19th century England DAVID COPPERFIELD, OLIVER TWIST

Falling down a rabbit hole ALICE

The organ recital; the mechanical wizard; a wild imagination JANE MOFFAT *(The Middle Moffat)*

A spy HARRIET *(Harriet, the Spy)*

1773 Boston; an apprentice to a silversmith JOHNNY TREMAIN

Colonial Wethersfield, Conn KIT TYLER *(The Witch of Blackbird Pond)*

Quarreling twins in 4th grade MITCH AND AMY

Adventurous spirit; getting into trouble; 30 bugs; scientific experiment; unfriendly Indian OTIS SPOFFORD

Kristie and the cold ELMER AND EINER

The Indian, Allesandro RAMONA

Scoliosis DEENIE

Freckles ANDREW *(Freckle Juice)*

98. Guess the Title

My students always enjoy guessing titles of books. I prepare 5 x 7 index cards with a summary of the fiction title. Upon their visit to the library (class), I read the cards. Students become very excited when they recognize a book title, and are eager to reveal it. Many of the titles chosen may not be as familiar to the children, however, I do mention that if they have not read the book, they are missing out on a good book. Titles which are appropriate to grade level, of course, are presented, and classic titles as well as very popular books, and new books are plugged.

99. What Animal Am I?

This activity can be used as a bulletin board activity or with a class coming to the library. I have used it with classes, and it sparked interest in titles that were mentioned, although children in the elementary school always are fond of animal stories. I say the name of the animal; the students say what type of animal it is (a lion, a dog, an elephant).

Grades 1-3

Anatole (*Anatole*, Titus): MOUSE
Dodo (*Little Monkey*, Thayer): MONKEY
Curious George (*Curious George* Books, Rey): MONKEY
Sammy (*Sammy the Seal*, Hoff): SEAL
Sam (*Sam Squirrel Goes to the City*, Dugan): SQUIRREL
Dinny (*Dinny and Danny*, Slobodkin): DINOSAUR
Day; Night (*Day and Night*, Duvoisin): DOG; OWL
Kippie (*Kippie the Cow*, Gretor): COW
Boo (*Boo*, Barry): COW
Little Maverick (*Little Maverick*, Coates): COW
Chester (*The Cricket in Times Square*, Selden): CRICKET
Crosspatch (*Crosspatch*, Evers): LION
Dandelion (*Dandelion*, Freeman): LION
Sylvester Duncan (*Sylvester and the Magic Pebble*, Steig): DONKEY
Gus (*Sam and the Firefly*, Eastman): FIREFLY
Mr. Roo; Ms. Boo; Jiffy (*Jiffy, Miss Boo and Mr. Roo*, Brothers): ROOSTER-CHICKEN; CAT; DOG
Uncle Analdas (*The Tough Winter-Rabbit Hill*, Lawson): RABBIT
Mittens (*Mittens*, Newberry): CAT
Horton (*Horton Hatches the Egg*, Seuss): ELEPHANT
Harry (*Harry and the Lady Next Door*, Zion): DOG
Orlando (*Orlando the Brave Vulture*, Ungerer): VULTURE
Thistle (*Thistle*, Zistle): RACCOON
Tammy (*Tammy Chipmunk and his Friends*, Allen): CHIPMUNK
Barney (*Barney Beagle Plays Baseball*, Bethell): DOG
Hugo (*Hugo the Hippo*, Baum): HIPPOPOTAMUS
Obash (*Birthday for Obash*, Chalmers): HIPPOPOTAMUS
Quack (*Little Quack*, Woods): DUCK
Willie (*Willie Duck*, McAuley): DUCK
Gertie (*Gertie the Duck*): duck
Angelique (*Angelique*, Janice): DUCK
Louise (*The Ambitious elephant*, Wood): ELEPHANT
Wumpy (*Wumpy's Christmas Gift*, Nash): ELEPHANT
Frances (*Bedtime for Frances*, Hoban): BADGER
Babar (*Babar Loses His Crown*, De Brunhoff): ELEPHANT
Scatter (*Scatter the Chipmunk*, Coblentz): CHIPMUNK
Johnny Town-Mouse (*The Tale of Johnny Town-Mouse*, Potter): MOUSE

[Game 99, continued]
Sylvester (*Sylvester, the Mouse with the Musical Ear*, Holl): MOUSE
Bernard (*Baseball Mouse*, Hoff): MOUSE
Snippy and Snappy (*Snippy and Snappy*, Gag): MOUSE
Timothy (*Timid Timothy: the Cat who Learned to Be Brave*, Williams): CAT
T-Bone (*T-Bone, the Baby Sitter*, Newberry): CAT
Corky (*Corky Learns a Lesson*, Ludvik): CHICKEN
Marco (*The Travels of Marco*, Merrill): PIGEON
Grizzwold (*Grizzwold*, Hoff): BEAR
Clyde (*The Guard Mouse*, Freeman): MOUSE
Mutt (*Mutt*, Bradbury): DOG
Clifford (*Clifford's Halloween*, Bridwell): DOG
Arthur Cluck (*The Strange Disappearance of Arthur Cluck*, Benchley): HEN
Smudge (*Smudge*, Newberry): CAT
Sheba (*April's Kittens*, Newberry): CAT
Scaredy Cat (*Scaredy Cat*, Krasilovsky): CAT
Nell (*Kitten Nell*, Bruna): CAT
Sneakers (*Sneakers*, Brown): CAT
Copy Kitten (*All About Copy Kitten*, Evers): CAT
Mac (*Night Cat*, Black): CAT
Pickles (*The Fire Cat*, Averill): CAT
Jenny (*Jenny's First Party*, Averill): CAT
Larry (*Larry the Canary*, Averill): CANARY
Smokey (*Smokey the Bear*, Watson): BEAR
Little Black (*Little Black, a Pony*, Farley): HORSE
Oscar (*Oscar Otter*, Benchley): OTTER
Katy (*Katy No-Pocket*, Payne KANGAROO
Timothy (*Timothy Turtle*, Graham): TURTLE
Mew; Purr (*Listen, Listen*, Ylla): CATS
Adelaide (*Adelaide*, Ungerer): KANGAROO
Little Red (*A House for Little Red*, Hillert): DOG
Rags (*Rags' Day and Mrs. Silk*, Hoke): DOG
Kitty (*A Little Dog Called Kitty*, Thayer): DOG
Top (*The No-Bark Dog*, Williamson): DOG
Robert (*Robert the Rose Horse*, Heilbroner): HORSE
Petunia (*Petunia*, Duvoisin): GOOSE
Jasmine (*Jasmine*, Duvoisin): COW
Crocus (*Crocus*, Duvoisin): ALLIGATOR

Parsley (*Parsley*, Bemelmans): DEER
Ben (*Dinosaur Ben*, DeCaprio): DINOSAUR
Lyle (*House on East 88th Street*, Waber): CROCODILE
Chin Ling (*Chin Ling, the Chinese Cricket*, Stilwell): CRICKET
George; Martha (*George and Martha*, Marshall): HIPPOPOTAMI
Chatterduck (*Chatterduck and the Plump Pig*, Evers): DUCK
Willie Waddle (*Willie Waddle*, Carter): DUCK
Ping (*Story about Ping*, Flack): DUCK
Hamilton Duck (*Hamilton Duck's Springtime Story*, Getz): DUCK
Peter (*The Tale of Peter Rabbit*, Potter): RABBIT
Bunny Fitfiddle (*The Fitfiddles Keep Fit*, Steiner): RABBIT
Daddy Long Ears (*Daddy Longears*, Kraus): RABBIT
Tiny Cottontail (*The Littlest Rabbit*, Isaacson): RABBIT
Angus (*Angus and the Cat*, Flack): DOG
Tico (*Tico and the Golden Wings*, Lionni): BIRD
Frederick (*Frederick*, Lionni): MOUSE
Anansi (*Anansi, the Spider*, McDermott): SPIDER
Light-Foot; Quick Foot (*No Fighting, No Biting*, Minarik): ALLI-
GATORS
Marshmallow (*Marshmallow*, Newberry): RABBIT
Hubert (*Hubert's Hair-Raising Adventure*, Peet): LION
Veronica (*Lonely Veronica*, Duvoisin): HIPPOPOTAMUS
Flip (*Flip and the Morning*, Dennis): HORSE
Porky (*Cowboy Sam and Porky*, Chandler): HORSE
Lucille (*Lucille*, Lobel): HORSE
Miss Hattie (*Miss Hattie and the Monkey*, Olds): MICE
Nora (*Little Nora*, Wells): MOUSE
Henry (*Henry*, Vreeken): MOUSE

Grades 4–6

Kristie (*Kristie Goes to the Fair; Here Comes Kristie*, Brock): HORSE
Tiss (*Tiss Takes a Trip*, Bialk): HORSE
White Prince (*White Prince, the Arabian Horse*, Tousey): HORSE
Flicka (*My Friend Flicka*, D'Hara): HORSE
Rosie (*Old Rosie, the Horse Nobody Understood*, Moore): HORSE
Midnight (*Midnight, a Cow Horse*, Meek): HORSE
Basil (*Basil of Baker Street*, Titus): MOUSE
Jeremy (*The Jeremy Mouse Book*, Scarry): MOUSE
Limpy (*Limpy, the Tale of a Monkey Hero*, Matzdorff): MONKEY

[Game 99, continued]
Robi; Hanni (*High in the Mountains*, Brock): MOUNTAIN LIONS
Old Ben (*Old Ben*, Stuart): SNAKE
Black Beauty (*Black Beauty*, Sewell): HORSE
Calico (*Catch Calico!*, Aaron): CAT
Polonius (*Polonius Penguin*, Abrahams): PENGUIN
Gareth (*Time Cat*, Alexander): CAT
Bobcat (*Bobcat*, Anderson): HORSE
Alf (*How the Witch Got Alf*, Annett): DONKEY
Comanche (*Comanche*, Appel): HORSE
Sounder (*Sounder*, Armstrong): DOG
The Runner (*The Runner*, Annixter): HORSE
Piebald (*National Velvet*, Bagnold): HORSE
Thomas (*Thomas the Ship's Cat*, Baker): CAT
Granny Fox (*The Adventures of Old Granny Fox*, Burgess): FOX
Mr. Fox (*Fantastic Mr. Fox*, Dahl): FOX
Ginger (*Ginger Pye*, Estes): DOG
Walter (*Walter, the Lazy Mouse*, Flack): MOUSE
Savage Sam (*Savage Sam*, Gipson): DOG
Old Yeller (*Old Yeller*, Gipson): DOG
Misty (*Misty of Chincoteague*, Henry): HORSE
Smoky (*Smoky*, James): HORSE
Bun (*Bun, a Wild Rabbit*, Lippincott): RABBIT
Little Georgie (*Rabbit Hill*, Lawson): RABBIT
White Fang (*White Fang*, London): DOG/WOLF
Moby Dick (*Moby Dick*, Melville): WHALE
Datra (*Datra the Muskrat*, Russell): MUSKRAT
Stuart (*Stuart Little*, White): MOUSE
Charlotte (*Charlotte's Web*, White): SPIDER
Mrs. Piggle-Wiggle (*Mrs. Piggle-Wiggle*, MacDonald): PIG
Flyk (*A Dog for Davie's Hill*, Bice): DOG
Man O'War (*Man O'War*, Farley): HORSE
Black Stallion (*Black Stallion's Courage*, Farley): HORSE
Amigo (*Amigo*, Cooper): HORSE
Giff (*Sara and the Winter Gift*, Mason): RACCOON
Haunt Fox (*Haunt Fox*, Kjelgaard): FOX
Vulpes (*Vulpes, the Red Fox*, George): FOX
George; Herbert (*George and Herbert*, McAuley): CROWS
White Bird (*White Bird*, Bulla): CROW
Herman (*Herman the Brave Pig*, Mason): HOG

Paddington (*Paddington on Top*, Bond): BEAR
Chandler (*Chandler Chipmunk's Flying Lesson & Other Stories*, Martin): CHIPMUNK
Tomas (*Follow Tomas*, Hurd): PELICAN
Petros (*An Island for a Pelican*, Fenton): PELICAN
Squawky (*Squawky; the Adventures of a Clasperchoice*, Potter): PARROT
Awk (*Awk*, Foreman): PARROT
Amos (*Ben and Me*, Lawson): MICE
Camembert; Roquefort; Gorgonzola (*Camemberg*, DeAngelis): MICE
Bitsy (*Bitsy*, Scott): CAT
Noodle (*Mr. Twitmeyer and the Poodle*, Adelson): DOG
Chip (*Chip, the Dam Builder*, Kjelgaard): BEAVER
Polynesia (*The Voyages of Doctor Dolittle*, Lofting): PARROT
Reddy; Granny (*Old Granny Fox*, Burgess): FOX
Zorra (*Zorra*, Franklin): FOX
Louis (*The Trumpet of the Swans*, White): SWAN
Sinbad (*Sinbad the Cygnet*, Unwin): SWAN
Socks (*Socks*, Cleary): CAT
Tim (*Tim, a Dog of the Mountains*, Johnson): DOG
Maxie (*Maxie*, Kahl): DOG
Butterball (*Terrible Mr. Twitmeyer*, Moore): DOG
Buck (*The Call of the Wild*, London): DOG
Petey (*Puppy Who Wanted a Boy*, Thayer): DOG
Big Mutt (*Big Mutt*, Reese): DOG
Black Stallion (*Black Stallion Revolts*, Farley): HORSE
Justin Morgan (*Justin Morgan Had a Horse*, Henry): HORSE
Smoky (*Smoky, the Cow Horse*, James): HORSE
Alexander (*Alexander's Birthday*, Knight): HORSE
Dan Domingo (*Dan Domingo; the Medicine Hat Stallion*, Henry): HORSE
Cocoa (*Cocoa*, Otto): HORSE
Wilbur (*Charlotte's Web*, White): PIG
Manhattan (*Manhattan Is Missing*, Hildick): CAT
Smokey (*Smokey the Well-Loved Kitten*, Goudey): CAT
Moumouth (*Nine Lives or the Celebrated Cat of Beacon Hill*, Fenton): CAT
Xerxes (*The Turnabout Trick*, Corbett): CAT
Spooky (*Suddenly a Witch!*, Bowen): CAT
Yaller Eye (*Yaller Eye*, Bell): CAT

Jenny Linsky; Edward; Checkers   (*Jenny's Adopted Brothers*,
    Averill): CATS
Sea Star (*Sea Star; Orphan of Chincoteague*, Henry): HORSE
Ralph (*Runaway Ralph*, Cleary): MOUSE
Rosalie (*Rosalie the Bird Market Turtle*, Lubell): TURTLE
Candy (*Hurry Home, Candy*, DeJong): DOG

100. Alice in Wonderland Tea Party

The characters of Lewis Carroll's *Alice in Wonderland* —
Alice, the Cheshire Cat, the Mad Hatter, the Queen of Hearts, the
Hare, the Dormouse, TweedleDee and TweedleDum — are represented by students in the class, and seated around a table. Each
student converses as the character represented. Each character
speaks about himself telling the others a little about the character
portrayed, and asks questions of the other characters. The remaining class members draw an invitation to the tea party out of a box.
Fantasy characters from well-known fantasy titles are selected, and
the student represents and mimics whichever character's name appears on the invitation drawn. The original Alice in Wonderland
characters take turns inviting another fantasy character to their
tea party from a guest list given to them by the librarian. To insure
the success of this activity, the students are each given a profile sheet
on the character ahead of time in order that they may be familiar
enough to carry on a brief conversation. The activity is most successful with grades 3 and up. Good characters are those from such books
as *Pinocchio* (Collodi); *The Magic Finger* (Dahl); *James and the
Giant Peach* (Dahl); *Charlie and the Chocolate Factory* (Dahl);
Winnie-the-Pooh (Milne); *Poor Stainless* (Norton); *Charlotte's Web*
(White); *The Lion, the Witch and the Wardrobe* (Lewis). Students
may simply read from their profile sheet if they have a problem
making up a conversation.

101. Truth or Consequences

This activity consists of telling the truth by answering a question correctly, or else paying the consequences. The librarian asks each student of the class one question, and the questions may be asked until all students except one has paid the consequences. Consequences may be placing dunce stickers on foreheads.

102. The Wind in the Willows Picnic Party

Similar to "Alice In Wonderland Tea Party." Invitations are given to animal characters. Characters include: Mr. Mole; Mr. Water Rat; Mr. Toad; etc.

103. Shadow Plays

Similar to puppet plays. Shadow puppets are made from thin cardboard or wood with handles attacked to allow manipulation. A rear-lighted white cloth or milk-plastic screen is set up, and what are seen from the front are sharply focused moving shadows.

104. Holiday Parties

Class parties are organized around holiday themes. Readings from holiday books: poems, stories; short plays; and non-fiction selections concerning the meaning of holidays, and how people celebrate them, and also customs of holidays around the world may be given by the librarian and/or the class members. Appropriate decorations enhance the atmosphere.

105. Bookmark Contest

All the grades may participate in this contest. The librarian may choose the most creative and most attractive bookmark(s) from each room. The winners are laminated and displayed in the library.

106. World Convention

Each class member becomes a delegate from a foreign country upon reading a non-fiction selection on a country. Each delegate relates to the other class members facts about his country, such as fascinating places to visit, or information of interest about customs, food, traditional dress or dances. Each delegate may show photographs.

107. Flannel Board

The younger children enjoy storytelling via the flannel board, and they may wish to tell a story by moving the flannel characters around themselves.

108. Yarnspinning Convention

Each member of the class relates a chosen story to the other members. Fiction, short stories, tall tales, fairy tales, folk tales, myths or legends are selected by the students to relate to the class. Students may read short segments from their selections.

109. Picture Parade

The lower grades (K–2) enjoy parading around the school dressed as storybook characters. Halloween costumes or simple adaptations may be worn with name tags identifying the storybook character.

110. Regional Americana

This topic calls to attention the many books written with the setting located in a particular region or particular state of the United States. The feeling and flavor of the place can be experienced by the reading of the book. An exhibit is set up showing such fiction books. Labels of states are arranged on a bulletin board with their state flags (optional: flags may be made by students). A book-jacket cover may be placed under the state name to serve as an example of regional Americana. Each member of a class may select one state, read one book with the setting of that particular state. Students may later report observations regarding objects mentioned, places, customs that appeared to be peculiar to that region or state.

111. Joke-Telling Festival

Books on jokes and riddles may be displayed. Students may select their favorites, and read them to the class upon visiting the library. A joke-telling festival may be announced to the 5th and 6th grade groups. Students select one joke or riddle to be told to the class with the teacher's and librarian's approval. The festival is held in the library for 20 to 30 minutes.

112. Character Alphabet

This activity is best suited for 4th grade and up. The librarian or a student leader calls a letter in the alphabet. Each student must think of a storybook character which begins with that letter. The students may write down their answers on a sheet of paper with the student having the most character names written down at the end of the exercise being the winner. Or a variation of this game is to ask one student at a time, going around the entire class to name a character with a specific letter. If the student cannot do this, he is out of the game. The remaining student who has named a character correctly without taking more than 20 seconds is the winner.

113. Navy Book Promotions

Students read books to earn their promotions. In order to join the navy, the student must read five books. Thereafter, pupils must read a specified number of books to be promoted until the very highest honor is awarded to the students who earn Admiral. 5 books earns entry to the Navy as ENSIGN; 10 books earns LIEUTENANT; 15 books earns COMMANDER; 20 books earns rank of CAPTAIN; 25 books promotes to COMMODORE; and 30 books earns rank as ADMIRAL. All Admirals have their names announced on the radio station, and also posted in the hallway.

114. Leapfrog

A number of Caldecott Award winning books are selected for a particular class. Each student gets one book. Students may be blindfolded to choose a book from the assortment on a table. Each student will then read the book chosen, and then give it to the person who sits in front of him. The next student reads it, and then passes it forward again. Each member of the class reads all the Caldecott selections.

115. Authors Card Game

I played this game when I was just a little girl, and perhaps it was my introduction to the titles and authors of classic books. I loved it then, and students seem to enjoy it now. The object of the game is to get as many "books" as possible by asking a player if he has a certain book. If that player possesses the book, he must give it to the player who asks for it. The player has a "book" when he receives all four components or titles by the same author. The librarian must have at least four to five packs of "Authors" for use with an entire class.

116. Misty Gala

Hold a Misty Gala with a poster of Misty of Chincoteague along with a display of the book, and comments by students who have read the story. The comments should encourage the reading of the book by others, and serve as advertisements to a reading of the story: one or two chapters a day may be read by the librarian or good student reader. The special reading should be announced and advertised to the school well ahead of time.

117. Student Readers

The upper grade students, grade 7 and up, may be selected to form a storytelling group. They may read stories to the lower grades (children relate well to other children). Or they may video tape a story; do a play; make a slide and cassette show or puppet show for the lower grades. The program, one will fine, stimulates an interest for those books.

118. Reading Club

A reading group can be organized for direct interaction with the librarian or teacher. Students must become members of the club by reading three books. They must record a brief summary on a 3 x 5 card, and present these to the librarian who reviews the cards. The librarian may then give acceptance to their admittance to the group. The students may go on to read other books, gaining recognition as they read. For example, five books may gain them a certificate; 10 books, a medal; 20 books, a letter of recognition from the school; 25 books, a trophy or a gift certificate, etc. Prizes may come from proceeds of a book fair, donations, or any other project.

119. Newspaper or Newsletter

The Library Club or a committee of students may wish to include in the school newspaper (if there is one), a column or section

pertaining to the library. Or else a newsletter may be planned each
month to tell the school about the great new books that have come
in; who won a specific contest; which class got to take Petunia to
their room; the upcoming activities slated for the library; and any
other news that would spark interest and business.

120. Puppetry

Students can make puppets or marionettes, and present them
in a scene from a book. All aspects of the theater could be studied
here. A simple puppet theater may be designed by arranging a
screen on a stand in the front of the room, in front of a doorway or
window. The screen should be large enough to hide the operators.
A wooden or cardboard box can be used for the stage. It should be
open to the front audience, and closed on the top and sides. Also,
it should be partially open at the bottom to allow puppets to be
positioned from underneath. A curtain across the front stage could
be assembled with pull cords for easy opening and closing. Students
could paint scenic backgrounds on paper so that the scenes can be
changed. Three-dimensional scenes may be created by placing objects (trees, furniture, model cars, etc.) on the stage. A filmstrip
projector or other lighting may be used for an effective spotlight.
Sound effects or music increases the reality of the program. Perhaps the library will wish to keep these presentations on video tape
for further use.

121. Guess the Book: Slide Show

A fun way of becoming familiar with illustrations and books
is to have a slide show of famous examples of illustrations from picture books. Often one can buy these, but the librarian can make
them by doing a little photography work in the media center.
Choose a number of classic illustrations from picture books. Equip-
ment needed: a copy stand and camera; a sheet of glass, preferably
the non-reflecting type; and photo flood lights. The extra work in-
volved here is worth it since it is easier to have the class focus on a
screen than try to show the students an illustration from a book, one
at a time. Also, the librarian can make various points, and not lose
half the class at the same time.

122. Radio Broadcast

A group of students may be responsible for reading the "news bulletin" for the day; or the radio broadcast may be a monthly event. Students may select their favorite books, or new books may be reviewed by a book reviewing committee. These reviews or bulletins are read over the radio station to alert the school of the book's existence.

123. History of Books

Students can make an exhibit for the library or hallway to show the school the history of books. They could make models of and draw illustrations of the early forms of books, writing utensils, and printing presses. Models of quills, brushes, and reeds may be displayed as well as the oldest type of books made from clay tablets. The art class could devise an example. A "papyrus" roll could also be made for display. Early books in America such as Benjamin Franklin's *Poor Richard's Almanac* may be illustrated, along with a student's hornbook. Examples of old and modern books, and paperbacks should be displayed. Each model or illustration should have an explanation, and a brief story of the history of books should be given. A group of students may work on the exhibit cooperatively. The librarian may select a committee of interested students who will work on this project.

124. Library Basketball

This activity can be used to reinforce reference skills or card catalog skills or in developing a desire for reading. A wastepaper basket can be set up on a desk or chair, and styrofoam or wadded paper used to make balls. A list of questions can be made up: reference questions; questions about the card catalog; or questions pertaining to books. The class may be divided up into two teams; team A getting asked a question; and then team B being asked a question. Whenever a question is answered correctly, the team gets a chance to shoot a basket, and if they get it in, receive a point. The winning team makes the most baskets, and likewise, the most points.

125. Author by Author; Illustrator by Illustrator; Title by Title; Character by Character

Portraits of authors, illustrators, or characters from books are passed around the class. The one who guesses the most wins this game.

126. Savings Bank

A savings bank is set up in the library. Students cash in on each book read by getting "money" for each book read. Certain categories of books may be labeled or ticketed as more expensive than others. Or else each book could be worth the same amount of money. For example, the bank could give out $100 for each book read. The student tries to get as rich as he can. Students must present a 3 x 5 card with a synopsis of the book, and an opinion of the book in two or three sentences. Upon giving the "banker" the card, the student receives a bill of money. The winner is the richest student at the end of a marking period. Records of money earned are kept by students in their library folders. The "money" is given to the librarian as evidence of a "balanced checkbook" before the winner is announced.

127. Listening to Newbery Award & Caldecott Award Medal Winners

One of the Caldecott or Newbery Medal Award winning books may be heard on a record, or make a tape cassette of your own by having members of the class read it (or at least one scene). Also, a tape cassette could be made consisting of a number of segments from a number of books with the class having to recognize the book from which the segment was taken.

128. Pantomime Rhyming

The class may be divided into two groups for this activity, team A and B. One team must leave the library in order to choose an author's name or a book character. Then the team comes back, and pantomimes every word the students can think of that rhymes with the chosen book character or author's name. This exercise is a little more difficult, and should only be used with the upper grades. It may be successful with the brighter students.

129. Book Border

Another way of giving credit for reading books is to make a four-page booklet with two leaves. Colored paper may be used. The books may be dressed up and decorated as much as desired. The student can write the title and author of the book read, and then write his or her own name in the lower right-hand corner. The booklets may vary in size, and extend around the room.

130. Blindman's Bluff

Form a circle and someone is chosen to be "it." Whoever is chosen must dig into a box containing questions or call numbers, or other such library skill activity. The person chosen "it" must then proceed to find the book that will answer the question, or find the book with the particular call number picked. The librarian may choose who will be "it."

131. Rebus

The rebus has been a perennial favorite with my classes. They love guessing the titles of books. I select titles of books from our library, and find magazine pictures that suggest phrases, words or parts of words, in the title (*see also* Activity No. 94). The following are some of the puzzles that I constructed—partly of pictures, partly of letters, words or syllables. Children ask to do this activity again and again.

The Jungle Book (The JUNGLE + BOOK)
Freckle Juice (BOY WITH FRECKLES + GLASS OF ORANGE JUICE)
Charlotte's Web (BUILDING LOTS + WEB)
The Hundred Dresses (100 DRESSES)
Around The World In 80 Days (A GLOBE + in 80 Days)
The Cave Twins (The CAVE + TWINS)
Treasure Island (TREASURE CHEST + ISLAND)
The Summer of the Swans (The SUMMER SCENE of the SWANS)
Ginger Pye (GINGER STICKS + PIE)
Black Pearl (Black PEARLS)
Kidnapped (A CHILD + A MAN NAPPING)
Watership Down (SEA SCENE + SHIP + Down)
Gulliver's Travels (SEAGULL iver's Travels)
Onion John (ONION + John)
Across Five Aprils (A CROSS + 5 + Aprils)
Teacup Full of Roses (TEACUP Full of ROSES)
Waterless Mountain (WATER less MOUNTAIN)
Hans Brinker HANDS Brink R)
Why the Sun and the Moon Live in the Sky (Y the SUN + MOON
  live in the SKY)
Pinocchio (PIN + OAK + KEY + O)
Socks (SOCKS)
Farmer Boy (FARMER + BOY)
Thunder Road (Thunder + ROAD)
The Animal Family (The VARIOUS ANIMALS Family)
Rollerskates (ROLLERSKATES)
White Sails to China (WHITE SAILS OF A SHIP + 2 + CHINA DISH)
The Mask (The MASK)
A Christmas Carol (A XMAS TREE + PRESENT + MUSIC SHEET)
Five Little Peppers (5 little PEPPERS)
The Beech Tree (The BEACH SCENE + TREE)
Fantastic Mr. Fox (FAN tastic Mr. FOX)
Smoky (SMOKE COMING OUT OF A STACK + E)
Here Comes Kristie (H + EAR Comes Kris TEA BAG or BOX OF TEA)
The Thanksgiving Story (THE PILGRIMS or THANKSGIVING SCENE
  + STORE + E)
Julie of the Wolves (JEWEL + E of the WOLF + S)
Island of the Blue Dolphins (ISLAND of the Blue DOLL + FINS)
The Door in the Wall (The DOOR in the WALL)
Henry Huggins (HEN + ry TEDDY BEARS HUGGING + ins)

White Fang (BLANK WHITE SQUARE + MAN WITH FANG)
Cricket in Times Square (CRICKET in X SQUARE)
Thimble Summer (THIMBLE + SUMMER SCENE)
Skates (ICE SKATES or ROLLER SKATES)
Little Women (Little WOMEN)
Mrs. Piggle Wiggle (Mrs. PIG + L Wiggle)
Shadow of a Bull (2 BULL HEADS FACING EACH OTHER)
Rabbit Hill (RABBIT + HILL)
Rufus M. (HOUSE WITH ROOF VIEW + US M)
Caddie Woodlawn (K D WOODPILE + LAWN)
The Long Winter (The Long WINTER SCENE)
The Strawberry girl (STRAWBERRY + GIRL)
Huckleberry Finn (BERRIES + FIN OF FISH)
The Wheel on the School (The WHEEL on the SCHOOL)
A wrinkle in Time (A WRINKLED FACE OF AN OLD WOMAN in time)
Trumpeter of Krakow (TRUMPET + er of Kra + COW)
The Twenty-one Balloons (The 21 BALLOONS)
Crow Boy (CROW + BOY)
Riding the Pony Express (Riding the PONY Express)
Once a Mouse (Once a MOUSE)
Whose Mouse Are You? (WHO-O-O S MOUSE R U)
I Wish I Wish (EYE wish EYE wish)
The Gingerbread Man (the GINGERBREAD MAN)
Frog Went a-Courtin' (FROG went a-courtin')
Happy Lion Roars (HAP + E LION Roars)
Castle (CASTLE)
The Pie and the Patty Pan (The PIE and the patty PAN)
Spaceship under the Apple Tree (SPACE CAPSULE under the APPLE TREE)
The Rooster Crows (The ROOSTER crows)
Song of the Swallows (MUSIC NOTES of the BIRDS)
Twig (TWIG OF A TREE)
Sam Bangs and Moonshine (Sam Bangs and MOON LIGHT RAYS EMANATING)
Springtime for Jeanne Marie (SPRING SCENE + CLOCK 4 Jeanne Marie)
Little Pear (Little PEAR)
(A Story a Story (A + STORE E A STORE E)
A Horse Called Lightning (A HORSE called LIGHTNING)
Drummer Hoff (DRUM R Hoff)

Jeannie's Hat (Jen KNEES HAT)
Stone Soup (STONE + CAMPBELL'S SOUP CAN)
Goggles (GLASSES)
Blueberries for Sal (BLUEBERRIES 4 Sal)
Sneakers (SNEAKERS)
The Biggest Bear (The Biggest BEAR)
ABC Bunny (A-B-C BLOCKS + BUNNY)
One Fine Day (One Fine DAYTIME SCENE)
The Story of the Three Bears (The Story of the 3 BEARS)
The Littlest Auto (The littlest CAR)
The Three Little Pigs (The 3 Little PIGS)
The Stupids Step Out (The POT OF STEW + pids STEPS out)
Arrow to the Sun (ARROW to the SUN)
umbrella (UMBRELLA)
Toad and Frog are Friends (TOAD + FROG R Friends)
Whistle for Willie (WHISTLING BOY 4 Willie)
Millions of Cats (Millions of CATS)
Make Way for Ducklings (Make Way 4 DUCK + lings)
Fish is Fish (FISH is FISH)
Petunia (PETUNIA FLOWER)
Clear the Track (Clear the TRAIN TRACK)
Snowy Day (SNOW SCENE Day)
The Egg Tree (The EGG + TREE)
The Little Island (The Little ISLAND)
Marshmallow BOY WITH A PACKAGE OF MARSHMALLOWS)
The Big Black Horse (The Big BLACK HORSE)
The Big Snow (The Big SNOW SCENE)
A Tree Is Nice (A TREE Is Nice)
The Cat in the Hat (The CAT in the HAT)
The Tale of Peter Rabbit (The TAIL of Peter RABBIT)
The Little House (The Little HOUSE)
In the Forest (In the FOREST SCENE)
Cat and Dog (CAT and DOG)
The King's Stilts (The KING'S STILTS)
Crocus (CROCUS FLOWER)
Sylvester and the Magic Pebble (Syl + VEST + er and the MAGI-
    CIAN DOING MAGIC + STONE)
Pedro of Olvera Street (Pay Dro of I'll vera STREET)
Ballet Shoes (BALLET SLIPPERS + SHOES)
Stuart Little (POT OF STEW + ART Little)

Betsy and the Circus (BET + SEA and the CIRCUS)
The Wind in the Willows (The WINDY SCENE in the WILLOW TREE)
David Copperfield (DAY SCENE + vid COPPER + FIELD)
Witch of Blackbird Pond (WITCH of BLACKBIRD + POND)
Ivanhoe (EYE + VAN + HOE)
Walter the Lazy Mouse (WALL + ter the laz + E MOUSE)
James and the Giant Peach (James & the GIANT PEACH)
Charlie and the Chocolate Factory (Char Lee & the CHOCOLATE + FACTORY)
Why Mosquitoes Buzz in People's Ears (Y MOSQUITOES Buzz in PEOPLE'S EARS)
The Witches of Worm (The WITCH + es of WORM)
Boy of the Pyramids (BOY of the PYRAMIDS)
Calico Bush (CALICO + BUSH)
Elf Owl (ELF + OWL)
Skyblazer (SKY + FIRE + er)
Castle on the Border (CASTLE on the BORDER SCENE)
Master Skylark (MAST + er SKY + LARK)
The Ark (The ARK)
Rowan Farm (ROWING + FARM)
Blue Mystery (BLUE + LITTLE GIRL + tery)
Mystery of the Fat Cat (LITTLE GIRL + TERY of the fat CAT)
Miss Hickory (LITTLE GIRL + HICKORY NUT)
The Secret in the Wall (The C + cret in the WALL)
Eagle Feather (EAGLE + FEATHER)
White Bird (WHITE SQUARE + BIRD)
Riders of the Storm (RIDERS of the STORMY SCENE)
The Ghost of Windy Hill (The GHOST + WINDY HILL SCENE)
The House of Thirty Cats (The HOUSE of 30 + CATS)
Five Boys in a Cave (5 BOYS in a CAVE)
Fifteen (5 + th TEENAGER)
Secret of the Andes (C + cret of the AND + D's)
The Fog Boat (The FOGGY SCENE + BOAT)
I Am a Mouse (EYE am a MOUSE)
Lord Jim Low + Rd J + hmmmmm)
Miracle on 34th Street (MIRROW + acle on 34th STREET)
Candle Tale (CANDLE + TAIL)
The Wild Little House (The Y + ild Little HOUSE)
Crimson Moccasins (Crim Son MOCCASINS)
A Toad for Tuesday (A TOAD for 2's + DAY)

The Matchlock Gun (The MATCH LOCK + GUN)
Tiger Burning Bright (TIGER + FIRE Bright)
Mystery of the Musical Umbrella (Mystery of the MUSIC + UM-
BRELLA)
Christmas Tree on the Mountain (XMAS TREE on the MOUNTAIN)
A Lantern in the Window (LANTERN in the WINDOW)
Harriet the Spy (HAIR E ET the Spy)
The Ghost of Five Owl Farm (The GHOST of 5 OWL + FARM)
Brady (BRAID + E)
The Ghost Downstairs (The GHOST Down + STAIRS)
Big Blue Island (Big Blue ISLAND)
Old Yeller (Old YELLOW SQUARE + er)
Little Men (Little MEN)
Elephant Boy of Burma ELEPHANT + BOY of Burma)
Dwarf Long Nose (DWARF Long NOSE)
Easter Fires (EASTER FIRES)
Shark Boy (SHARK + BOY)
Sea Star (SEA + STAR)
The Gift of the Magi (The GIFT of the Magi)
Henry 3 (HEN + ry 3)
The Arm of the Starfish (The ARM of the STARFISH)
Cotton in My Sack (COTTON in My SACK)
The Wonderful Boat (The Wonderful BOAT)
The Hundred Penny Box (The 100 PENNY + BOX)
Bats and Balls (BATS and BALLS)
The Black Stone Knife (The Black STONE + KNIFE)
Sand (SAND)
River of the Wolves (RIVER of the WOLVES)
The Black Tiger (The BLACK SQUARE + TIGER)
The Snake That Went to School (The SNAKE That Went to SCHOOL)
Dogs of Fear (DOGS of F + EAR)
Iron Cage (IRON + CAGE)
The Secret of the Rosewood Box (The Secret of the ROSE + WOOD
    + BOX)
Clues in the Woods (CL + oooooohs in the WOODS)
Today I Am a Ham (2 + DAY EYE Am a HAM)
Tucker's Countryside (TUCK + er's COUNTRY SCENE Side)
Ash Road (ASHES + ROAD)
Flaming Arrows (FLAMES + ing ARROWS)
The Black Arrow (The BLACK SQUARE + ARROW)

13 Ghosts (13 GHOSTS)
The Red Lion (The Red LION)
Circus Shoes (CIRCUS + SHOES)
Skating Shoes (SKATES + ing + SHOES)
The 13 Clocks (The 13 CLOCKS)
Many Moons (MAN E + MOONS)
The New Girl (The New GIRL)
The Watch House (The WATCH + HOUSE)
The Question Box (The ? BOX)
Hot on Ice (Hot on ICE)
Frogs Merry (FROGS Merry)
The First Peko-Neko Bird (The 1st Peko-Neko BIRD)
Once There Was a Kitten (Once there was a KITTEN)
Mabel the Whale (May + BELL the WHALE)
Peter's Chair (Peter's CHAIR)
Monkey Day (MONKEY + DAY)
Lucille (Lu SEAL)
Ladybuy, Ladybug! (LADYBUG + LADY + BUG)
The Duck on the Truck (The DUCK on the TRUCK)
The Little Airplane (The Little AIRPLANE)
The Attic Witch (The ATTIC + WITCH)
Pear-Shaped Hill (PEAR-shaped + HILL)
Mouse Tales (MOUSE + TAILS)
The Rice-Cake Rabbit (The RICE + CAKE + RABBIT)
Swimmy (SWIMMING + E)
No Fighting, No Biting (No FIGHTING, No BITING)
Little Red Nose (Little Red NOSE)
Ants Are Fun (ANTS R Fun)
Time of Wonder (CLOCK of Wonder)
The Funny Little Woman (The Funny Little WOMAN)
Little Bear (Little BEAR)
The Secret Three (The Secret 3)
Crickets and Frogs (CRICKETS and FROGS)
The Snowflake and the Starfish (The SNOWFLAKE and the STAR-
     FISH)
Mittens (MITTENS)
The Box with Red Wheels (The BOX with Red WHEELS)
The Boats on the River (The BOATS on the RIVER)
Seven Diving Ducks (7 DIVING + DUCKS)
The Guard Mouse (The GUARD + MOUSE)

Little Toot (Little 2 + oot)
The Three Goats (The 3 GOATS)
A House for Little Red (A HOUSE for small red paper square)
The Boy with a Drum (The BOY with a DRUM)
Robins and Rabbits (ROBINS and RABBITS)
At The Seashore (At the SEASHORE)
Some Day (Some DAY)
The Pecan Tree (The PEA + CAN + TREE)
Benny's Nose (Ben + EEES NOSE)
The Horse That Takes the Milk Around (The HORSE That Takes
    the MILK Around)
Sparrow Socks (SPARROW + SOCKS)
The Bug that Laid the Golden Eggs (The BUG that laid the Golden
    EGGS)
The Shadow Book (The SHADOW + BOOK)
The Mitten (The MITTEN)
Pierre (PEA + air)
Two Too Many (2 2 MAN E)
The Tomato Patch (The TOMATO patch)
The Brave Cowboy (The Brave COWBOY)
Willow Whistle (WILLOW TREE + WHISTLE)
900 Buckets of Paint (900 BUCKETS of PAINT)
Red Fox and his Canoe (Red FOX and His CANOE)
The Alphabet Tale (The ABC + TAIL)
Harry the Dirty Dog (HAIR + E the Dirty DOG)
The Big Golden Animal ABC (The Big Golden ANIMAL ABC)
Parsley (PARSLEY)
The Toad Hunt (The TOAD Hunt)
Run, Zebra, Run (Run, ZEBRA, Run)
I Saw a Ship A-Sailing (EYE Saw a SHIP A-Sailing)
Too Many Dogs (2 MAN EE DOGS)
Cowboy Small (COW + BOY small)

132. Literary Lotto

This game is played with cards. Each player or student has
five blank cardboard or laminated color paper markers, half an inch
square. Each student also has a literary lotto card. Prepare a list of

book characters, or titles, for the librarian. Arrange the book characters, or titles in a different order on each card. The librarian calls
a book character, and each student covers the identical character
with a marker. The game is won by the first student to cover five
squares in a row, and he calls LOTTO!

133. Discussion of a Specific Topic in Fiction

Very often, a student is interested in reading a number of cat
stories or horse stories, or whatever it is she likes. I have often held
mini-sessions on showing and telling students about various topics
found in fiction books such as books on animals; Caldecott Award
winners; regional Americana; Indian and pioneer days; holidays;
funny books; books about problems and conflicts with parents,
adults, teachers, relatives, friends; tall tales; books on seasons;
fairy tales; imagination books; machines personified; stories about
the ancient world; national heroes; folk tales; Newberry Award
winners; mystery and detective stories; adventure; fantasy; science
fiction; sports stories; travel and books of foreign settings; historical
fiction; myths and legends; and sea stories; witches and supernatural; other lands and people; romance; self-understanding; and
the list goes on and on. I have to laugh when students fight over a
book that I have shown to them. This is easily enough settled by a
number game which we play. I think of a certain number in my
head. If there are 10 students who want to take out a specific book,
and there is only one copy of it in the library, they guess by taking
turns, what the number is in my head, from one to ten. This is a
fair way of giving the book to one of them.

134. Hangman

The class may be divided into two groups for this one. Anything can be used, such as a title, author, illustrator, character, and
the librarian writes on a blackboard as many dashes as there are in
the letters in the word or words. A letter may be called, and if the
guess is correct, the librarian fills in the spaces wherever it appears
in the word or series of words. If the guess is wrong, the librarian

begins to draw the scaffold, man, and may go so far as to draw eyes, nose, etc. After presenting this activity, ask if anyone has read the book (if titles are presented), or if the class knows any other books by a particular author of illustrator.

135. Petunia Day

In order to stimulate interest in the library and the responsibility of returning books by the due date, a Petunia Day (Anansi, the spider, Peter Rabbit, or any other popular book character) may be promoted. Petunia is placed on a special shelf or special place in the library. She could be made out of cardboard, or made into a stuffed figure. When a class brings all the books back without forgetting even one, the class gets to take Petunia back with them to their room to visit for the week. If the class brings every book back to the library on the next visit, they can keep Petunia for another week, otherwise, she must be returned to the library. (The librarian must keep a number of Petunias in case more than one class has a perfect score.) At the end of the year, the class who had Petunia for the most weeks wins a party, and is given something special.

136. Book Report Contest

This contest could be held over a period of time, like a marking period, or one month's time. A number of books are selected of varying lengths, difficulty, and theme for a particular grade or class. Each book in the contest is assigned a specific point value from one to five with a colored sticker or tape attached to each book. A student selects a book to read, and then selects one of five book report activities displayed on the bulletin board. Activities can include: designing book jackets; making an exhibit or model from a scene of the book; drawing a scene or sequence of scenes from the book; doing a traditional book report by filling out a form; or creating their own ending to the story. Upon completion of reading the book, and doing the activity, the student receives points from one to three, or one to five. These points are added to the original point value assigned to the book. These statistics are filled in a chart. The student with the most points wins, and is given a prize. A party is held.

137. Book Elections

Reading can be fostered by holding book elections. Classes or individual groups can vote on favorite books, authors, illustrators, book characters, etc. by caucus. A meeting can be held to nominate favorites. Nominating and seconding speeches can be given. The entire school or a class could vote on their favorites. A victory party can be held after the elections.

138. Alphabet Game

Each student of the class comes to the library prepared with a paper and pencil. The librarian or a student leader names the letter of the alphabet, and each student writes the name of as many authors as he can that begin with that letter. Titles of books, illustrators, or book characters can be used.

139. Tic Tac Toe

This activity game can be played with two people or with two groups of people. Instead of putting X's and O's in the boxes, the group that puts in the X's can instead write in a famous animal character, for example, and the O's can instead write in a famous human character. Or the X's can write in a title of a book, and the O's can write in a famous author.

140. Charades

This is always a fun activity for the classes, although more successful with the upper grades. The class could be divided into two groups, with one group trying to guess what the other group is presenting. Or one student could present a charade to the class. Characters of books, titles of books, famous illustrators, or authors may be used for this activity. Examples of titles that may be used are: *Fifth Down* (Allen); *Caddie Woodlawn* (Brink); *Pinocchio* (Collodi); *Heidi* (Spyri); *Hot on Ice* (Woolgar); *Across the Tracks*

(Young); *Space Cat* (Todd); *Hans Brinker* (Dodge); *Ivanhoe* (Sir Walter Scott); *Kidnapped* (Stevenson).

141. Character; Title; Author

The class sits in a circle for this one. One student stands or sits in the center with a soft ball (could be made out of paper or foam). The player in the center must throw the ball to a student in the circle, and at the same time, say either "CHARACTER," "TITLE," or "AUTHOR." If the center player says "CHARACTER," the player who catches the ball has five to 10 seconds (whatever the time limit set) to name a character in a book. If he fails to do so, he is out of the game. The person who is left wins the game. Or a variation of this could be that the librarian be the center player, and throws the ball to the circle of students.

142. Fishing in the Frog Pond

All grade levels enjoy this game, but especially the younger levels — 1, 2, and 3 — love it. A fishing pole and pond is made out of cardboard or a cardboard box is decorated with blue tissue paper. The object of this game would be to catch a fish (a book title in the shape of a fish, frog, toad or other such frog pond inhabitant). The student would retrieve the book from the shelf, read it, and later tell the class whether or not it was a "good catch."

Grades 1-3

Fish Is Fish (Lionni)
A Fish Out of Water (Palmer)
Swimmy (Lionni)
Deep Sea Farm (Ipcar)
McElligot's Pool (Seuss)
Lizard's Song (Shannon)
Little Toad to the Rescue (Shortall)
Tyler Toad and the Thunder (Crowe)
Frog Band and Durrington Dormouse (Smith)
Turtles' Picnic and Other Nonsense Stories (Bergen)

Great Frog Swap (Roy)
Jump, Frog, Jump! (Kalan)
Moon, Stars, Frogs and Friends (Maclachan)
Turtle (Cummings)
Lizard Lying in the Sun (Freschet)

143. Book Jacket Jigsaw Puzzle

I have taken book jackets from classic, well-known and popular books; laminated them; cut them into puzzle pieces for use with the younger grade special education groups, and the younger grades. They enjoy this activity very much, and it often leads them to take out the book itself.

144. Students Illustrate Their Stories

We have had students draw and color or paint book characters which the younger grades especially like to do, although I could not always decipher who the character was supposed to be. Then we would have a parade of characters with the children trying to guess the book character. They always enjoy this.

145. Students Write a Story

Many children really do, I find, like to create and write down stories, and some have been very good. I notice that the younger grades 1, 2, and 3 especially like this exercise, although often the upper grades 4, 5, and 6 may enjoy creative writing also. I will be given stories to read throughout the school year which the children have written themselves.

146. Books That Have Become Movies

Get a film from the public library, and show a short segment of it to interest students. Here are some movies that were made from books:

Watership Down
Charlie and the Chocolate Factory
Moby Dick
Treasure Island
David Copperfield
Twenty-thousand Leagues under the Sea
Gulliver's Travels
Eighty Days Around the World
Oliver Twist
The Red Balloon
Little House on the Prairie (TV series)
Pinocchio
The Wizard of Oz
Alice in Wonderland
The Last of the Mohicans
Robinson Crusoe
The Robe
Sherlock Holmes (TV)
Hardy Boys (TV detective series)
Mrs. Mike
The Old Man and the Sea
Les Miserables
Nancy Drew (detective series)
The Red Badge of Courage
Miracles on Maple Hill

147. True or False

This game is presented to the class upon visiting the library. The librarian prepares a list of true and of false statements pertaining to fiction books. Some of the false statements are quite preposterous and obvious. Other statements are more subtle in tone. Statements are made up from titles which the pupils have been checking out of the library, and also from classic and well-known books. The class is divided into two teams for this activity. The winner is the team that scores the most winning answers with one point being given for each correct answer.

148. Magazine Cutouts

Children may write a story, and select pictures from magazines that illustrate their story. Old magazines which students are permitted to use from home can provide beautiful and interesting illustrations. The student makes a book with a cover of colored construction paper and magazine pictures. The same procedure may be used with adapting an already familiar story, or fairy tale rather than creating an original story. The books are displayed in the library for all to see.

149. Best Book Ever

Students vote by ballot for their choice of the best book they read during that school year. Ballots are collected by three categories: grade 1–3; grades 4–6; and grades 7–8. The book that gets the most votes is displayed in the school showcase.

150. Passport to a Country

Upon reading a fiction selection, a student receives a "passport" to the country in which the book takes place. "Passports" with the student's name, and country visited, are placed on the wall or bulletin board.

Hills End (Ivan Southall) AUSTRALIA
Boy of the Pyramids; a Mystery of Ancient Egypt (Ruth F. Jones) EGYPT
The Lion of the Kalahari (Sam Hobson & George Carey) AFRICA
Boris (Jaapter) RUSSIA
Rowan Farm (M. Benary-Isbert) GERMANY
Little Baptiste (May McNeer) CANADA
Call It Courage (Armstrong Sperry) SOUTH SEAS
The Jungle Book (Rudyard Kipling) INDIA
Dogs of Fear (Musa Nagenda) AFRICA
Silk and Satin Lane (Esther Wood) CHINA
Good-bye Mr. Chips (James Hilton) ENGLAND

151. Treasure Hunt

This activity consists of posting a list of reference questions to be answered on a weekly basis. The student who comes up with all correct answers first is the winner, and is honored with a prize. Proceeds from donations or book fairs may be used to purchase prizes.

152. Library Lottery

A copy of a favorite book is the prize won in the library lottery. Students place their tickets into a receptable located in the hallway or in the library. The book could be purchased with donated money or proceeds from an event, or PTO funds, or other means. Sample books could include *Charlie and the Chocolate Factory* (Dahl); *James and the Giant Peach* (Dahl); *Charlotte's Web* (White); *The Lion, the Witch, and the Wardrobe* (Lewis); or any other favorite book. The librarian or principal may draw the winning ticket out of a receptacle after the tickets have been thoroughly mixed.

153. Haiku High Jinks

Upon hearing a reading of some of *Cricket Songs: Japanese Haiku* or *More Cricket Songs* translated by Harry Behn, the class writes their own verse of haiku. These may be read to the class on their next visit, although the librarian should not indicate which student wrote which verse, unless the children wish to be known.

154. Tall Tale Festival

Students gather in a circle to read various American tall tale stories from Paul Bunyan; John Henry; Johnny Appleseed; Johnny Inkslinger; Pecos Bill; Billy the Kid; David Crockett; Jesse James; and others. Students may vote on their favorite whopper. Students may also enjoy making up their own whopping tall tales with a little preparation.

155. Mark Twain Week

Various classes may partake in Mark Twain Week when selections of his works are read by students and/or the librarian, and comments made about the books by both. A film clip may be shown. Or students may perform a scene from one of the books depicting an interesting point. Quotes from the book may be selected for posters or signs advertising that Mark Twain Week is approaching.

156. Stifle, Sit & Read

A sustained silent reading program calls attention to reading and books. The principal may be of help in organizing such an activity for once a week. On this occasion, the entire school would stop what they are doing, sit quietly, and read for a prescribed period of time (15 minutes). Every student would be required to have a book for this reading period.

157. Ezra Jack Keats Week

Display the books of Ezra Jack Keats for a week. Children (grades 1 and 2) love the illustrations of these books. Classes may take books back to their rooms for the week. Discuss with the classes the techniques Mr. Keats uses to accomplish his art work. For example, the collage technique and the oil paints in a tub of water.

158. Anagrams

This activity can be used as a party game. Tables in the library are marked by various labels: authors; illustrators; titles; book characters; or more specific labels such as mystery writers; science fiction writers. Students may be paired off or they may progress in any one of three ways: (1) The winning duet moves up, and the losing duet would go to the last table; (2) All students move to another table; (3) Half the students move up, and the other half move back, and the students or players take turns turning up a letter.

The student who does the turning of a letter tries to name a book character, title of book, or author or illustrator (whatever is selected) beginning with that letter. At the authors table, a student must name an author, not a book character, etc. If the student cannot immediately answer, any other student at the table may try to answer. Unclaimed letters must lie face up, and can be claimed at any time. As soon as the players have made several progressions, they may get their categories mixed up. There are no penalties for these errors; however, a student is not, of course, allowed to pick up a K for saying "Kidnapped" at the author table.

159. Making a Book Project

Students may enjoy making a book. They can write individual or group stories, and illustrate them, neatly print or write a finished copy; threading it, and making an attractive cover. The books may be displayed throughout the school hallway or inside the library.

160. Dr. Seuss Week

Bartholomew, a character from a book in the collection of Dr. Seuss, may be selected to visit the grade 1 and 2 classrooms along with the Dr. Seuss collection. After one week, Bartholomew and the collection visit the next class.

161. Student Projects

Students can make: dolls; scenes from books; exhibits; posters; book friezes; bookplates; peep shows with scenes from books; engage in movie making (cartoons or scenes from books). Some of the art work could be done in collaboration with the art teacher.

162. Old Book Contest

In order to promote reading of books that have become tattered and worn looking, and in order to stimulate reading of all books in the library, students can choose books that have missing jackets, or are in need of outside repair. Once they are repaired, students design and make book jackets for them. They must also have read the book since they must write a brief summary on the inside flap besides making attractive illustrations for the cover. The entries are displayed, and judged by the librarian. One or more winning entries could be chosen with 1st place, 2nd place, and 3rd place. The jackets are used permanently, and prizes could be awarded.

163. Curious George Week

Curious George books may be featured for a week. Students may read as many titles as they can, and since the library will be depleted of a supply, each class (1st grade and 2nd grades) may exchange books. Students may take a poll on their favorite selection. Students may make up (orally) their own episode of a Curious George adventure.

164. Fables Fête

Books of fables are featured. A class is read a number of fables and after each one, pupils try to express the moral of the story.

165. Book Publishing

Pupils are selected to form an editorial staff in order to publish a book. Books may be made by the students as a contest, and the winning book gets to be published. The editor with the staff will have the responsibility of advertising for and selecting a book. They produce copies to distribute to the school.

166. Nursery Rhymes

Children in grades 1 and 2 enjoy recalling nursery rhymes. I have read some of the more well-known ones, and left out a word here and there. The children fill in the blanks with glee, and they like to hear the familiar verses over and over. I also read to them a few unfamiliar rhymes to whet their appetite for more.

167. Salesman

Students can select a favorite book and try to "sell" it to the class. Various sales techniques can be incorporated with the librarian's help. The student is successful if someone in the group or class wishes to take the book out to read. Students can get points and a "commission" with the books they "sell."

168. Folklore Fiesta

Books of folktales of countries around the world are exhibited under captions of the country. Dolls of foreign lands are placed beside the appropriate country caption. Read a folktale to the class from one of the books. Have each member of the class read one folktale from one of the countries upon taking the selections back with them to the classroom. The next time the class comes to the library, three or four students or the librarian may read a folktale from a collection.

169. Humor Holiday

A number of humorous books — fiction; limericks; nonsense verses; and stories — are displayed. When the class visits the library, each student may relate to the others about the book read, or read from a couple of nonsense verses or limericks that were thought hilarious. Students can then make a plug for their book by advertising it to the rest of the school with signs or posters about their funny selection.

170. Poetry Party

Students may compose their own poetry, and have it displayed in the library. Students in a class may also select one of their favorite poems to be read to the rest of the class. Students can vote on their favorite poem heard, and also the favorite poem written by their classmates.

171. Story Collections Jubilee

Each student in the class reads one short story. Each one thereupon tells it to the class in brief. The librarian may select a short story to read to the class.

172. Potpourri

To celebrate National Book Week or Children's Book Week or any other special event, the librarian may advertise any number of contests and activities. For example, an author or illustrator of children's books may be invited to visit the school; or students may guess how many books are in their school library. Choose prizes for the winners.

173. Battle of the Books Quiz Program

Two teams are formed for this game. Students devise at least three questions about fiction books read, that they ask the other students. The first person in team A asks the first person in team B a question. Then the first person in team B asks the second person in team A a question, alternating down the line. The team that answers the most questions receives the most points, one point for each correct answer, and wins the game. A variation of this is to have the first person of team A ask any member of team B a question (a free for all). The team with the most correct answers and points wins.

174. Fairy Land

Each student of a class reads one fairy tale, and upon coming to the library gives a summary of the story.

175. Bookworm Ball

After reading a book, each student of a class becomes the character in the book. For example, upon reading *Alice in Wonderland*, a student may become the part of Alice, or any of the other characters in the book. All the book characters are written on a piece of paper, and put into a box. Each student will draw from the box one piece of paper. If the pupil selects his own character, he must put it back, and select another slip. The character which is drawn must converse with the pupil who picked it (30 seconds to one minute) by asking questions of the character, and holding a conversation appropriate to the book character. One student selects a slip of paper from the box at a time, and then talks with the book character that was selected.

176. Dive for Pearls

Oyster shells are made out of construction paper, oak tag, cardboard or other material. Inside the shells are placed "pearls" or titles of books written on paper, and then folded to form a pearl. In front of the oysters are cards with brief summaries of fiction books. Upon the class visit to the library, each student writes down what he believes to be the title of the books. One student is asked to read the titles to the class from the "pearls." The student who guesses the most titles, and therefore collects the most number of "pearls" wins this contest.

177. Go to the Head of the Class

Upon the class visit to the library, students are asked questions dealing with the library: regarding fiction or non-fiction books;

card catalog; Dewey Decimal Classification System; reference questions; library skills. The librarian asks one student at a time a question. If the student answers it correctly, then he goes to the head of the class (stands in front of the room). All the class members are asked a question. The students who answer incorrectly are out of the game. Students who answer correctly are then asked questions until only one student is left standing at the head of the class. This activity is much like a spelling bee. The children always enjoy it.

178. Kaleidoscope

The students are seated except for four to six class members who stand in front of the group. This game may be correlated with authors, titles, book characters or illustrators. Each of the four to six students are given the name of an author, or title of a book, or book character, or illustrator. The class is not told the author, title of book, book character, etc. which the students represent. The four to six students are given profile sheets to read to the class which tell about themselves, or about a particular title. The class must guess the author's name, illustrator, book character, or title of book which each student represents. A variation of this game is to have the class be given a list of authors, titles, or characters that would correlate with the profile sheet given to the students. The object would be to match titles with authors, or characters with titles.

179. Cross Questions

Cross Questions is very successful with my classes. Ever since I first used this activity (especially with grades 1, 2, and 3, but with the older groups as well), the children have pestered me to allow them to play this. They love this one! Try it, and watch the enthusiasm. Like a spelling bee, have the class divide into two teams, A and B. Ask questions of each student, alternating teams. A correct answer earns one point for the team. I tell the teams that any talking will insure the team to lose a point while the other team gains a point. If four consecutive pupils cannot answer the question, or answer incorrectly, the question is eliminated. The team with the most points at the end of a specified time period wins the contest.

Grades 1–3

What animal is Petunia? GOOSE
What animal is Veronica? HIPPOPOTAMUS
How many cats did an old man bring home to his wife? MILLIONS
What kind of animal is Angus? DOG
How many hats did Bartholomew Cubbins take off? 500
What kind of pet did Archie bring to the pet show? GERM IN A JAR
In *The Snowy Day*, what did Peter do with the snowball? PUT IT
IN HIS POCKET
In *The Little House*, why was the house sad? BECAUSE SHE WAS IN
THE MIDDLE OF A BIG, DIRTY, NOISY CITY
In *The Tale of Petter Rabbit*, what did Peter do to get into mischief?
WENT INTO MR. MACGREGOR'S GARDEN
What is the name of Mike Mulligan's steam shovel? MARY ANN
What animal does the Indian boy meet in *The Mighty Hunter?* BEAR
"Little Black" is what kind of animal? HORSE
"Sneakers" is what kind of animal? CAT
Who is Jasmine? COW
Snippy and Snappy are what kind of animals? MICE
Madeline gets sick in the book, *Madeline*. What is wrong with her?
APPENDIX
What kind of animal is Parsley? DEER, AN OLD STAG
What is curious George constantly doing? GETTING INTO MISCHIEF
Who is Babar? AN ELEPHANT
In the book, *In the Forest*, what musical instrument does the little
boy blow? HORN
What did Mary Ann, the steam shovel, become at the end of the
book, *Mike Mulligan and His Steam Shovel?* FURNACE
Who is Periwinkle? GIRAFFE
What was Petunia's treasure? TRUNK WITH A ROCK IN IT
Where did Petunia take a trip? TO THE CITY
What is Little Silk? A JAPANESE DOLL
In *Here Comes Kristie*, what is Kristie? HORSE
Who is Pika? A ROCK RABBIT
In *Snowy and Woody*, who is Brown Bear? WOODY Which one is
Polar Bear? SNOWY
In *Andy and the Lion*, how did Andy help the lion? PULLED OUT A
BIG THORN
In *A Fish Out of Water*, what did the little boy name his fish? OTTO

In *Blue Bug to the Rescue*, what does Blue Bug warn his bug friends? NEVER TO TASTE OR EAT POISONOUS PLANTS

What happened to the fish in *A Fish Out of Water*? HE GREW TOO BIG FOR HIS BOWL

In the book, *The Big Snow*, how do the animals find food? PEOPLE PUT OUT FOOD TO HELP THEM

Who is Crocus? A CROCODILE

What happens to Crocus' teeth? PULLED OUT, AND GETS FALSE ONES

In *Veronica and the Birthday Present*, what is the present? WHITE KITTEN WITH BLUE EYES

What is Loopy? AIRPLANE

What is Little Toot? TUGBOAT

What didn't Ferninand, the bull, want to do? BE PICKED TO FIGHT AT THE BULLFIGHTS IN THE GREAT ARENA

In *Alexander and the Wind-Up Mouse*, what does Alexander want? HE WANTS TO BE A WIND-UP MOUSE LIKE WILLY, AND BE CUDDLED AND LOVED

Who changed Willy, the wind-up mouse into a regular mouse? A LIZARD

Who is Minette? A CAT

In the book, *Why Mosquitoes Buzz in People's Ears*, who started all the trouble? THE MOSQUITO

In *Make Way for Ducklings*, what were Mr. and Mrs. Mallard looking for? A PLACE TO MAKE THEIR HOME

Who is Emmett? A DOG

When do the swallows come back to Capistrano in California in the book, *Song of the Swallows?* MARCH 19TH or ST. JOSEPH'S DAY

What does Marco tell his father in *And to Think That I Saw It on Mulberry Street?* LIES ABOUT WHAT HE SEES ON HIS WAY HOME FROM SCHOOL

Who was Harry in *Harry and the Lady Next Door?* DOG

What does the bunny look for in *The Bunny Who Found Easter?* EASTER WHERE HE HOPES TO FIND OTHER BUNNIES FOR COMPANY

What does Max do in *Where the Wild Things Are?* GOES OFF TO AN IMAGINARY LAND OF MONSTERS

Who is Pippa? A MOUSE

Which fiction books tell the adventures of a bunch of 2nd graders who have fun, go on picnics, have secrets, get into mischief? "BETSY & EDDIE" books by Carolyn Haywood

Grades 4–6

What is the Newbery Prize? BEST BOOK OF THE YEAR
What is the Caldecott Prize? BEST PICTURE BOOK OF THE YEAR
Who wrote *A Christmas Carol?* CHARLES DICKENS
What kind of animal is White Fang? PART WOLF, PART DOG
What is Moby Dick? WHITE WHALE
Who wrote *Treasure Island?* ROBERT LOUIS STEVENSON
What was Pinocchio? PUPPET
What kind of animal did Jody find in *The Yearling?* FAWN
Who was Huckleberry Finn's friend? TOM SAWYER
What kind of animal characters are in *Watership Down?* RABBITS
Who writes books that take place in India, and he was born in India
    also? RUDYARD KIPLING
Who is the real-life person who tells the stories in the *Little House
    on the Prairie* series? LAURA INGALLS WILDER
What is the name of Dorothy's dog in *The Wizard of Oz?* TOTO
What is the fantasy about tiny people who have their homes behind
    partitions in old houses, and manage to live by borrowing all
    kinds of little objects? *THE BORROWERS*
Who is an English nursemaid? MARY POPPINS
What are the names of the two main characters in *Return from
    Witch Mountain* and also *Escape to Witch Mountain?* TIA and
    TONY
What can Dr. Dolittle do that is different? TALK TO THE ANIMALS
What state did the Ingalls family move to in *Little House on the
    Prairie?* KANSAS
A leatherstocking tale about frontiersmen, Indians, the English, and
    the French? THE LAST OF THE MOHICANS (by James Fenimore
    Cooper)
The book, *My Brother Sam Is Dead*, by James Lincoln Collier takes
    place during which war? U.S. REVOLUTIONARY WAR
The book, *The Red Badge of Courage* by Stephan Crane took place
    during which war? CIVIL WAR
Who wrote *Uncle Tom's Cabin?* HARRIET BEECHER STOWE
Who wrote *The Mouse and the Motorcycle?* BEVERLY CLEARY
Who wrote *Freckle Juice?* JUDY BLUME
"Runaway Ralph" is what animal? MOUSE
What is the name of the cricket in *The Cricket in Times Square?*
    CHESTER

"Sea Star" and "Misty" are what kind of animals? HORSES
"Paddington" is what kind of animal? BEAR
Edgar Allan Poe writes what kind of stories? SCARY: TERROR
20,000 Leagues Under the Sea takes place in a? SUBMARINE
"Ginger" in *Ginger Pye* is what kind of animal? DOG
The name of a book by Donald Sobol which gives quickie mysteries
   which clues are provided and the reader is challenged for a solu-
   tion? TWO-MINUTE MYSTERIES
Sherlock Holmes is a famous? DETECTIVE
In *Manhattan Is Missing*, who is Manhattan? A SIAMESE CAT
Finish this title: *Boy of the Pyramids, a Mystery of Ancient?* EGYPT
Carolyn Keene writes what kind of books? MYSTERY
In the book, *Around the World in 80 Days*, how does the main char-
   acter travel? BALLOON
In Lamorisse's *The Red Balloon*, how did Pascal take a trip around
   the world? THE BALLOONS CAME DOWN FROM THE SKY AND
   CARRIED HIM AWAY
In the book, *Goodbye, Mr. Chips* by James Hilton, what does Mr.
   Chips do? PROFESSOR
What kind of books does Andre Norton write? SCIENCE FICTION

Part IV
Fun with Book Lists

180. Crafts Carnival

Craft books may be exhibited: macrame, weaving, sewing, model-making, needlepoint, paper maché, art from found objects, cardboard crafts, etc. Examples of student craft work may be displayed here. Various local craftspeople may be invited to display their crafts in the library.

181. Careers Carousel

A number of career books are presented in a display, along with a copy or copies of *Occupational Outlook Handbook*. People from various career fields may be invited to visit the library, and discuss their work with students. Students can be given the opportunity to ask questions.

182. Rainbow Round-Robin

Two or more classes may try to find as many titles as possible with a color as part of the title. These could be posted on the bulletin board under the class. Students could use the card catalog, go to the public library, or find titles any way they can. The winning class produces the most titles.

Green Says Go (Emberley)
Color Seems (Haskins)

Color of His Own (Lionni)
Tico and the Golden Wings (Lionni)
One Little White Shoe (Gezi)
What Color Am I? (Nye)
Is It Red? Is It Yellow? Is It Blue? (Hoban)
Pinkish, Purplish, Bluish Egg (Peet)
Greentail Mouse (Lionni)
Colors Are Nice (Holl)
Red Balloon (Lamorisse)
*Gray Goose and Gander: And Other Mother
   Goose Rhymes* (Rockwell)
Blue Bug's Treasure (Poulet)
Pink Pink (De Lage)
The Yellow Boat (Hillert)
Purple Mouse (MacIntyre)
Blue Bug and the Bullies (Poulet)
Blue Thing (Pinkwater)
Mystery of the Magic Green Ball (Kellogg)
Mystery of the Missing Red Mitten (Kellogg)
Green Monday (Thomas)
White Sparrow (Brown)
Black Pearl (O'Dell)
Few Green Leaves (Pym)
Green Futures of Tycho (Sleator)
Summer of the Green Star (Lee)
Blue Mystery (Benary-Isbert)
Green is for Galanx (Stone)
Green Book (Walsh)
Yellow House Mystery (Warner)
Adventure at Black Rock Cave (Lauber)
Mystery of the Golden Ram (Malone)
Red Pawns (Wibberley)
Lavender-Green Magic (Norton)
Red Hart Magic (Norton)
Golden Arrow (Heck)
White Pony (Oldham)
Night the White Deer Died (Paulsen)
Blue Poodle Mystery (Hope)
The Black Tiger (O'Connor)

183. Name-Calling

The same procedure may be followed for this bulletin board activity as with the Rainbow Round-Robin.

Grades 1–3

Madeline (Bemelmans)
Sam, Bangs and Moonshine (Ness)
Maggie and the Pirate (Keats)
Katy No-Pocket (Fix)
Lucille (Lobel)
Broderick (Ormondroyd)
Frederick (Lionni)
Orlando the Brave Vulture (Ungerer)
Obadiah the Bold (Turkle)
Oscar Otter (Benchley)
Olly's Polliwogs (Rockwell)
Rosie's Walk (Hutchins)
Jamie's Story (Watson)
Johnny's Egg (Long)
Max, the Music-Maker (Stecher)
Millicent (Baker)
Nini at Carnival (Lloyd)
David's Waiting Day (Watts)
Belinda's Ball (Bodger)
Clyde Monster (Crowe)
Geraldine, the Music Mouse (Lionni)
"No, Agatha" (Isadora)
Debbie Goes to Nursery School (Lenski)
Willie's Adventures (Brown)
Charles and Claudine (Berson)

Grades 4–6

Heidi (Spyri)
Adam of the Road (Gray)
Gulliver's Travels (Swift)
The Adventures of Tom Sawyer (Twain)

James and the Giant Peach (Dahl)
Huckleberry Finn (Twain)
Charlie and the Chocolate Factory (Dahl)
Here Comes Kristie (Brock)
Oliver Twist (Dickens)
Ramona, the Brave (Cleary)
Alice in Wonderland (Carroll)
David Copperfield (Dickens)
Henner's Lydia (de Angeli)
Johnny Hong of Chinatown (Bulla)
Starring Sally J. Freedman as Herself (Blume)
Lady Ellen Grae (Cleaver)
Kathleen, Please Come Home (O'Dell)
Sara Summer (Hahn)
Kate (Little)
Secret Emily (Scism)
Fat Jack (Cohen)
Ms. Isabelle Cornell, Herself (Farley)
Sophia Scarlotti and Ceecee (Feagles)
Ann Aurelia and Dorothy (Carlson)
Kitty in the Middle (Delton)

184. Tally Ho!

Similar to Rainbow Round-Robin and Name-Calling.

Grades 1-3

Millions of Cats (Gag)
500 Hats of Bartholomew Cubbins (Seuss)
One Morning in Maine (McCloskey)
One Fine Day (Hogrogian)
*One Day I Closed My Eyes and the World
    Disappeared* (Bram)
One Monster after Another (Mayer)
Three Stalks of Corn (Politi)
Two Piano Tuners (Goffstein)
Three Wishes (Galdone)

Three Little Pigs (Galdone)
Three Sillies (Jacobs)
Two Lonely Ducks (Duvoisin)
One Step, Two (Zolotow)
Three Funny Friends (Zolotow)
One Was Johnny (Sendak)
Six Special Places (DeBruyn)
Two Dog Biscuits (Cleary)
One, Two, Where's My Shoe? (Ungerer)
Seven little Monsters (Sendak)
Little Devil's 1, 2, 3 (Asch)
GIA and the $100 Worth of Bubble Gum (Asch)
I Am Five (Fitzhugh)
Fifty Million Sausages (Benedictus)
One Monday Morning (Shulevitz)
*I Can Lick 30 Tigers Today and Other
   Stories* (Seuss)

Grades 4–6

The Twenty-One Balloons (DuBois)
The Hundred Dresses (Estes)
20,000 Leagues Under the Sea (Verne)
Around the World in 80 Days (Verne)
Five Little Peppers and How They Grew (Sidney)
Tale of Two Cities (Dickens)
Fifteen (Cleary)
65th Tape (Ross)
Sixth Winter (Orgill)
Seven Days in May (Knebel)
Zero Trap (Gosling)
Ninth Car (Rooth)
5 Minutes to Midnight (Shabtai)
Seven Games in October (Brady)
Twelve Is Too Old (Mann)
Two Bishops (Turnbull)
Three Wishes for Jamie (O'Neal)
Second Coming (Percy)
Three Women at the Water's Edge (Thayer)
30 For a Harry (Hoyt)

Second Generation (Fast)
Noon: 22nd Century (Strugatsky)
666 (Anson)
Thirteenth Hour (Lee)
Miracle on 34th Street (Davies)

185. Affinities

Similar to Rainbow Round-Robin.

Grades 1–3

George and Martha (Marshall)
George and Herbert (McAuley)
Crickets and Frogs (Mistral)
Jay and the Marigold (Robinet)
Blue Bug and the Bullies (Poulet)
The Porcupine and the Tiger (Powell)
John and His Thumb (Shortall)
Boris and His Balalaika (Slobodkin)
Sam, Bangs and Moonshine (Ness)
Show and Tell (Martin)
Jack and Jill (Alcott)
Charlie and the Chocolate Factory (Dahl)
Tall and Proud (Smith)
Tucker and the Horse Thief (Terris)
Sprout and the Dogsitter (Wayne)
Danny Dunn and the Swamp Monster (Williams)
Mitch and Amy (Cleary)
Beezus and Ramona (Cleary)
David and the Phoenix (Ormondroyd)
James and the Giant Peach (Dahl)

186. Witchery Contest

Similar to Rainbow Round-Robin, Name-Calling, and Tally-Ho. Or else use the same activity with one class to determine who in the class can find the most titles. This contest will not work when the entire class is in the library at the same time, with everyone trying to use the card catalog at the same time, so it should be done on an individual basis. Students may wish to go to the public library or the bookstore to gain titles.

Grades 1–3

How the Witch Got Alf (Evers)
Littlest Witch (Massey)
Witch Bazooza (Nolan)
City Witch and the Country Witch (Williams)
Grandpa Witch and the Magic Doobelator
    (Kessler)
Humbug Witch (Belian)
Jolly Witch (Burch)
Old Black Witch (Devlin)
Old Witch and the Polka-Dot Ribbon (Devlin)
Spotted Dog: The Strange Tale of a Witch's
    Revenge (Parker)
Teeny, Tiny Witches (Wahl)
Weather Witch (Stubbs)
Witch Who Lost Her Shadow (Calhoun)
Witch Who Was Afraid of Witches (Low)
Witches Four (Brown)
Witch's Garden (Postma)
Witch's Hat (Dermer)
Beware! Beware! A Witch Won't Share (DeLage)
Farmer and the Witch (DeLage)
Old Witch and Her Magic Basket (DeLage)

Grades 4–6

The Witch of Blackbird Pond (Speare)
April's Witches (Crook)
Witches of Worm (Snyder)
Suddenly a Witch (Bowen)
Witch of the Cumberlands (Stephens)
White Witch of Kynance (Calhoun)
Witch of Hissing Hill (Calhoun)

Witchfinder (Rayner)
Witch of Glen Gowrie (MacKellar)
April Witch and Other Strange Tales (Ireson)
River Witches (Shecter)
Witch's Sister (Naylor)
Witching Hour (Krensky)
Witch Water (Naylor)
Witch Herself (Naylor)
Rebel Witch (Lovejoy)
Letter, the Witch, and the Ring (Bellairs)
Because of the Sand Witches There (Steele)
*Active-Enzyme Lemon-Freshened Junior High
   School Witch* (Hildick)
Would Be Witch (Chew)
Witch's Garden (Chew)
Witch's Broom (Chew)
What the Witch Left (Chew)
Wednesday Witch (Chew)
No Such Thing As a Witch (Chew)

187. Food Feast

Similar to Rainbow Round-Robin. Also, a display could be
arranged for the titles that have been produced.

Grades 1–3

Marshmallow (Newberry)
The Egg Tree (Milhous)
Parsley (Bemelmans)
Truffles for Lunch (Berson)
Three Stalks of Corn (Politi)
Scrambled Eggs Super (Seuss)
Dandelion (Freeman)
Blueberries for Sal (McCloskey)
Where the Wild Apples Grow (Hawkinson)
Chicken Soup with Rice (Sendak)
Suzie Celery (Reed)

Apple to Eat or Cross the Street (Weissman)
Stone Soup (Brown)
Chicken (Weil)
If Eggs Had Legs: Nonsense and Some Sense (Weil)
World in the Candy Egg (Tresselt)
Lamb Who Went to Paris (Thayer)
Popcorn: A Frank Asch Bear (Asch)
Sand Cake: A Frank Asch Bear Story (Asch)
City Sandwich (Asch)
Good Lemonade (Asch)
Country Pie (Asch)
Johnny's Egg (Long)
Lucy Lemon (Reed)
Tom Tomato (Reed)

Grades 4–6

Strawberry Girl (Lenski)
Ginger Pye (Estes)
Onion John (Krumgold)
Five Little Peppers and How They Grew (Sidney)
James and the Giant Peach (Dahl)
Charlie and the Chocolate Factory (Dahl)
Wild Oats (Epstein)
Chocolate Touch (Catling)
Bunch from Bananas (Pownall)
Big Cheese (Bunting)
Eddie Spaghetti (Frascino)
Fiddler, the Fire, and the Feast (Robin)
Hoboken Chicken Emergency (Pinkwater)
Take Tarts as Tarts Is Passing (Clymer)
Uncle Lemon's Spring (Yolen)
Soup (Peck)
Fortune Cake (Jordan)
View from the Cherry Tree (Roberts)
Berries Goodman (Neville)
Stowaway to the Mushroom Planet (Cameron)
Jelly and the Spaceboat (Parenteau)
Jelly Belly (Smith)

Mrs. Fish, Ape, and Me, the Dump Queen
  (Mazer)
My Darling, My Hamburger (Zindel)
Superfudge (Blume)

188. Blooms and Greens

Similar to food feast.

Grades 1-3

Petunia (Duvoisin)
Crocus (Duvoisin)
Jasmine (Duvoisin)
Dandelion (Freeman)
Pussy Willow (Brown)
In the Forest (Ets)
Plant Sitter (Zion)
Three Stalks of Corn (Politi)
Periwinkle (Duvoisin)
Lentil (McCloskey)
Rose for Pinkerton (Kellogg)
Peony's Rainbow (Weston)
Blossom Bird Goes South (Paul)
Thistle (Zistel)
Wishing Tree (Chew)

Grades 4-6

Lottery Rose (Hunt)
Crocuses Were Over, Hitler Was Dead (Symons)
Miss Hickory (Bailey)
Mimosa Tree (Cleaver)
Poppy Seeds (Bulla)
Willow Whip (Brown)
Miracles on Maple Hill (Sorensen)
To the Tune of a Hickory Stick (Branscum)
Year of the Apple (New)
Sunflower (Sharp)

Lilac Night (Hinkemeyer)
Cloverdale Switch (Bunting)
Columbine (Kennedy)
Blue Willow (Gates)
Goldenrod (Towne)
Palm Sunday (Vonnegut)
Where the Red Fern Grows (Rawls)
Ash Staff (Fisher)
Tree in the Trail (Holling)
Don't Sit Under the Apple Tree (Brancato)

189. Titles That Have a Foreign Name

Similar to Food Feast.

Grades 1-3

Pantaloni (Bettina)
Moustachio (Rigby)
Gillespie and the Guards (Elkin)
Mr. Fong's Toy Shop (Politi)
Emile (Ungerer)
Adelaide (Ungerer)
Anatole (Titus)
Taro and the Bamboo Shoot (Matsuno)
Pierre (Sendak)
Leopold, the See-Through Crumbpicker (Flora)
Pezzettino (Lionni)

Grades 4-6

Luigi and the Long-Nosed Soldier (Slobodkin)
Beau Geste (Wren)
Uncle Misha's Partisans (Suhl)
Nikolenka's Childhood (Tolstoy)
Pepito's Speech at the United Nations (Moore)
Pedro the Angel of Olvera Street (Politi)
Tales of Mr. Pengachoosa (Rush)

Magdalena (Shotwell)
Miss Bianca: A Fantasy (Sharp)
And Now Miguel (Krumgold)
Pepe Moreno (Allen)

190. Titles with Month of the Year

Grades 1-3

December Tale (Sachs)
April Fool Mystery (Nixon)
April Fool! (Jacobs)
April's Kittens (Newberry)
May I Bring a Friend? (de Regniers)
October Fort (Hoban)

Grades 4-6

December Tale (Sachs)
March (Kuniczak)
April's Age (Russ)
April's Witches (Crook)
April Ghost (Hall)
June the Tiger (Fort)
July's People (Gordimer)
August the Fourth (Farmer)
April Spell (Hoppe)
September Storm (Abels)
One April Vacation (Wallace-Brodeur)
Across Five Aprils (Hunt)

191. Book Titles with a Day of the Week

Grades 1-3

Saturday I Ran Away (Pearson)
Sunday Morning We Went to the Zoo (Ray)

Saturday Morning Lasts Forever (Bram)
Monday I Was an Alligator (Pearson)
Friday Night Is Papa Night (Sonneborn)
Friday the 13th (Kroll)
One Monday Morning (Shulevitz)
Mr. Bumba's Tuesday Club (Harwood)
On Sunday the Wind Came (Elliott)

Grades 4–6

Freaky Friday (Rodgers)
The Saturdays (Enright)
A Toad for Tuesday (Erickson)
Wednesday Witch (Chew)
Sunday Punch (Newman)
Sunday Whirligig (Eiseman)
Welcome Sundays (Keifetz)
Sunday Cycles (Gault)
Saturdays in the City (Bond)
Saturday, the Twelfth of October (Mazer)
Wednesday the Rabbi Got Wet (Kemelman)
Thursdays, Til 9 (Trahey)
Fridays (Gauch)
*Friday and Robinson: Life on Esperanza
    Island* (Tournier)
Thursday's Child (Streatfield)

192. Homonyms: Titles That Can Have Two Meanings

Petunia (Duvoisin)
Crocus (Duvoisin)
Marshmallow (Newberry)
Sneakers (Brown)
Periwinkle (Duvoisin)
Snowy and Woody (Duvoisin)
Day and Night (Duvoisin)
Dandelion (Freeman)

Mittens (Newberry)
Thistle (Zistel)
Smudge (Newberry)
Hercules (Gramatky)
Manhattan Is Missing (Hildick)
Misty (Henry)
Socks (Cleary)
Smoky (James)
White Fang (London)
Catch Calico (Aaron)
National Velvet (Bagnold)
Miss Hickory (Bailey)
Ginger Pye (Estes)

193. Catch a Creepy Crawly

Anansi the Spider (McDermott)
Ladybug, Ladybug (Kraus)
The Lace Snail (Byars)
The Bug that Laid the Golden Eggs (Selsam)
Wolfie (Chenery)
Be Nice to Spiders (Graham)
Ants Are Fun (Myerick)
Fast Is Not a Ladybug (Schlein)
Snail, Where Are You? (Ungerer)
Blue Bug to the Rescue (Poulet)

194. Books That Begin with the Letter "B"

Students guess as many titles of books that they can think of that begin with the letter **B** (or any letter), and they may use the card catalog for this activity. This gives good practice in the use of finding title cards. Grades 3 and up could participate in this exercise.

Baby's House (McHugh)
Beebi, the Little Blue Bell (Gezi)
Belinda's Ball (Rodger)
Biggest Snowstorm Ever (Paterson)
Blue Thing (Pinkwater)
Bod's Dream (Cole)
Blue Bug to the Rescue (Poulet)
Book of Hugs (Ross)
Butterfly (Delaney)
Bubblebath! (Manushkin)
Bow Wow Meow: A First Book of Sounds (Bellah)
Biggest House in the World (Lionni)
Baby (Burningham)
Blanket (Burningham)
Big Red Barn (Brown)
Blackboard Bear (Alexander)
Boy, the Baker, the Miller and More (Berson)
Best of the Bargain (Domanska)
Bremen Town Musicians (Domanska)
Biggest Shadow in the Zoo (Kent)
Blueberries for Sal (McCloskey)
Butterflies Come (Politi)
Brookie and Her Lamb (Goffstein)
Bearymore (Freeman)

195. Name a Book Title

Individual project. Students must name a book title that they have read that begins with an assigned letter of the alphabet.

A *Anatole; Arrow to the Sun*
B *Babar Loses His Crown*
C *Cat and Dog*
D *Day and Night*
E *Egg Tree*
F *Finders Keepers; Fish Is Fish*
G *George and Martha*
H *Harry the Dirty Dog*
I *In the Forest*
J *John Henry: An American Legend*
K *King's Stilts*
L *Little Island*
M *Maggie and the Pirate*
N *No Fighting, No Biting*
O *Old Stump*
P *Parsley*
Q *Quiet! There's a Canary in the Library*
R *Red Fox; Rosie's Walk*
S *Sam, Bangs and Moonshine*
T *Tale of Squirrel Nutkin*
U *Under the Lemon Tree*
V *Velveteen Rabbit*
W *Walter the Lazy Mouse*
X *Xerus Won't Allow It*
Z *Zip Goes Zebra*

196. Hide and Seek

The librarian hands out call slips to one student at a time upon the class visit to the library. The student is given a time limit (20 seconds, say) to locate the book.

197. I Spy

The class is divided into four groups. Each group of students is given a list of questions and some clues of where to find the answers (reference books and books on the shelves). The group of detectives who first completes the task wins.

Part V

Library and Reference Skill Games

198. Living Call Numbers

Name a specific topic to be looked up in the card catalog. Each member of a group or class can be given a topic on a piece of paper. They write down the call number of the subject, and then proceed to look for it in the library as the librarian and teacher see to it that they have found the correct book. Or else, the call number may be written on a piece of paper, and the student must find the book in the library. Students seem to enjoy this exercise.

199. Hot Potato

As the class visits the library, a "hot potato" is passed around with a call number on it. The librarian throws the hot potato to the first student in a line, and the pupil must find the book with the call number in less than 10 to 15 seconds or he gets "burned." Then the hot potato is given to the next student in line. The object is not to get burned. The "hot potato" may be a real potato, or made from a small cardboard box with a call number taped onto it, or rolled up newspaper, or other material.

200. Hot–Cold

The librarian says the call number of a book, and each student in turn is asked to find that call number while the librarian tells them they're getting warmer or cooler as the student tries to find the book.

Index

Note: References are to item numbers